Disability and In
Early Years Ec

Disability and Inclusion in Early Years Education supports practitioners in understanding and implementing inclusive practice relating to disability in early years education. Offering a detailed explanation of recent developments in the field, such as the 2015 SEND Code of Practice, it provides straightforward and accessible guidance on implementing the crucial procedures that help to promote good practice.

More broadly, the book provides guidance on creating a fully inclusive early years environment that will support all children, focusing on high-incidence needs around communication, behaviour and learning. Chapters offer a wealth of practical tools and strategies to support the inclusion of children with disabilities more effectively, covering key topics such as:

- assessment, early identification and individualised learning
- working with parents, carers and families
- the key role of picture books
- multisensory approaches to learning
- supporting behaviour and communication

This text will be valuable reading for all early years practitioners and students who want to promote the inclusion of children with SEND in mainstream provisions.

Chris Collett is former Senior Lecturer in Early Childhood Education and Care at Newman University, UK.

Diversity and Inclusion in the Early Years

Disability and Inclusion in Early Years Education
Chris Collett

Gender Diversity and Inclusion in Early Years Education
Kath Tayler and Deborah Price

LGBT Diversity and Inclusion in Early Years Education
Deborah Price and Kath Tayler

Disability and Inclusion in Early Years Education

Edited by
Chris Collett

Routledge
Taylor & Francis Group

LONDON AND NEW YORK

First published 2018
by Routledge
2 Park Square, Milton Park, Abingdon, Oxon OX14 4RN

and by Routledge
711 Third Avenue, New York, NY 10017

Routledge is an imprint of the Taylor & Francis Group, an informa business

© 2018 selection and editorial matter, Chris Collett; individual chapters, the contributors

British Library Cataloguing-in-Publication Data
A catalogue record for this book is available from the British Library

Library of Congress Cataloging-in-Publication Data
Names: Collett, Chris (Christine), editor.
Title: Disability and inclusion in early years education / edited by Chris Collett.
Description: Abingdon, Oxon ; New York, NY : Routledge, 2018. |
    Includes bibliographical references.
Identifiers: LCCN 2017009031 | ISBN 9781138638273 (hardback) |
    ISBN 9781138638280 (pbk.) | ISBN 9781315637877 (ebook)
Subjects: LCSH: Children with disabilities—Education (Early childhood) |
    Inclusive education. | Special education. | Early childhood education.
Classification: LCC LC4019.3 .D57 2018 | DDC 371.9/046—dc23
LC record available at https://lccn.loc.gov/2017009031

ISBN: 978-1-138-63827-3 (hbk)
ISBN: 978-1-138-63828-0 (pbk)
ISBN: 978-1-315-63787-7 (ebk)

Typeset in Optima
by Apex CoVantage, LLC

Printed and bound by CPI Group (UK) Ltd, Croydon, CR0 4YY

To all the children and families, who, over the years, have allowed us – for a brief time – to share their extraordinary lives.

Contents

List of figures   ix
List of tables   x
List of contributors   xi

Introduction   1
CHRIS COLLETT

PART I
Principles of inclusion   **7**

1   **Why include children with SEND?**   9
     CHRIS COLLETT

2   **Assessment, early identification and individualised**
     learning   26
     SUE MITCHELL AND KAREN THORPE

3   **Working with parents, carers and families**   57
     CHRIS COLLETT

4   **Who can help?**   74
     CHRIS COLLETT

PART II
Creating an inclusive early years setting   **99**

5   **The key role of picture books and other resources**   101
     KAREN ARGENT

Contents

6 Supporting communication   121
CHRIS COLLETT

7 Multisensory approaches to learning   140
INGRID SMITH

8 Supporting behaviour   162
STEVE BROWN

Conclusion   191
CHRIS COLLETT

Appendix 1   193
Appendix 2   196
References   200
Index   207

Figures

1.1   The medical model   12
1.2   The social model   15
2.1   The continuum of need   37
2.2   The one-page profile   40
2.3   SEN support plan   50
4.1   Agents for the child   75
4.2   Changing dynamics of service sectors   78
5.1   Example of a picture book that includes a character
      with a physical disability   110
5.2   Picture books that include a character with ASD   111
5.3   Example of a picture book with no disability
      clues on the cover   114
6.1   Ideation, planning and execution   127
6.2   Triad of impairment   129
8.1   Conflict spiral   165
8.2   Example of an individual work station   169
8.3   Now and next board   173
8.4   Happy–anxious sliding scale   174
8.5   Talking low and slow, to allow processing time   183
8.6   Restricted choice   187

Tables

2.1   Methods of differentiation   38
2.2   Outcomes   43
2.3   The SMART target   45
7.1   Sensory experiences in the outdoor 'rainforest'   152
7.2   Sensory experiences in indoor activities   159

Contributors

Karen Argent is a retired lecturer in Early Childhood Education and Care (ECEC). Prior to this, she worked in a wide range of educational settings, and as an inclusion worker on one of the first Sure Start programmes. Her research interests include representations of diversity in children's literature and she is a co-founder of the Letterpress Project.

Steve Brown has worked in children's services and education for twenty years, both in the UK and Australia. He currently delivers training and school support to specialist and mainstream settings.

Chris Collett is a retired lecturer in Early Childhood Education and Care (ECEC), specialising in SEND and inclusion after having spent twenty-five years teaching children and young people with moderate to profound learning disabilities. She was then a local authority advisory teacher for children under 5 with SEND and an Area SENCO.

Sue Mitchell has been an Area SENCO for the past twelve years and also works at a Child Development Centre. Prior to this, she had taught in special schools and on the SEND teacher training programme in Uganda.

Ingrid Smith has over thirty years' experience in teaching across the full spectrum of learning disabilities, from pre-school to young adults. She specialises in teaching and leading practice with children with profound and complex needs.

Karen Thorpe has over twenty-five years' experience as a teacher for both Early Years and primary-age children with SEND. She currently leads a team of advisory teachers who deliver training and support the inclusive practice of SENCOs in Early Years settings.

Introduction
Chris Collett

Minimal coverage of special educational needs and disabilities (SEND) and inclusion during initial training means that early years practitioners often lack the confidence to effectively support these children and their families. Paradoxically, this is the crucial age at which many children with SEND are identified, and the value of prompt intervention has long been recognised. My experience as a specialist support teacher, Area SENCo and, more recently, teaching BA and foundation degree early years undergraduates, have all indicated the need for a comprehensive yet straightforward guide to including children with SEND that provides a clear policy context, explaining the rationale for inclusion, but is also a comprehensive resource to support good practice.

According to the 2015 Special Needs and Disability Code of Practice:

> All children are entitled to an education that enables them to: achieve the best possible educational and other outcomes, and become confident young children with a growing ability to communicate their own views.
>
> (DfE 2015:79)

The aim of this book is to make clear the rationale for inclusion, while providing current and future practitioners in early years settings with a range of practical tools and strategies that can be adapted to enable them to include children with disabilities successfully, at the same time supporting more effectively all the children in their care.

The terminology that describes disability in an acceptable way has changed over time and can be a source of some anxiety; there can be a fear of causing offence by saying the wrong thing. According to the Disability Discrimination Act (Great Britain 1995), now incorporated into the Equality Act (2010), a disability is an impairment that has a *substantial and long-term* effect on an individual's ability to carry out tasks of everyday life. Special educational needs, as defined in the 2014 Children and Families Act, refers to a young person who has a learning difficulty or disability which calls for special educational provision to be made for them. There is considerable overlap between these two definitions, and latterly the terminology commonly used in the legislation reflects this. For the purposes of this book, the term 'special educational needs and disabilities' (SEND), from the 2015 SEND Code of Practice, has been used. As the focus of this book is disability, unless otherwise stated, 'inclusion' refers to the inclusion of children with SEND in mainstream provisions. Early years settings, unless otherwise specified, refers to non-maintained settings in the private, voluntary and independent sector, although where appropriate, maintained early years settings, that is, local authority nursery schools, and nursery classes attached to schools, have also been included in the discussion. Early years practitioners refers to teachers and non-teachers working in the early years sector.

Although the principle of the inclusion of children with special needs and disabilities was established in the late 1970s, the practicalities of its implementation continue to be complex. Back then, I undertook a teaching degree in what was then called 'mental handicap' (what would now be termed learning disabilities). My fellow students and I were training for a career teaching in the special school sector. However, even as I was studying for my degree, changes were afoot, when, in 1978, the Warnock committee published their report, following the review of education for 'handicapped' children (DES 1978). And in 1981, the same year that I graduated, a landmark Education Act (DES 1981) based on the Warnock Report enshrined in law for the first time, the concept of 'integration', later to evolve into 'inclusion', for children with special needs and disabilities, giving them the right (subject to certain criteria) to be educated alongside their peers in a mainstream school.

Of course, change would not happen overnight, but it seemed inevitable that, having recognised the moral obligation, it could be only a matter of time before all those children who were at that time being educated in segregated special schools, quite separately from their peers, would be included instead in mainstream provision. Those of us who had trained specifically to teach in special schools, would either need to adapt or be out of a job. We need not have worried. Nearly forty years on, the special school sector in England, as in other industrial countries around the world, is going strong, and the number of children educated in segregated specialist provision has barely diminished. In 1981, there were 127,157 children placed in segregated special schools. In 2000, there were still 102,621 children in segregated special schools or referral units (Whittaker 2001). The 2012 schools census indicates that in 2012 there were 95,000 children in state or independent special schools, but a further 22,000 children in separate pupil referral units. The sharpest decline in special schools was between 1981 and 1991, and in recent years the advent of free schools has seen the opening of further segregated provision.

These figures must of course be seen in the context of the growing population overall, and it should be noted that the population of children in specialist provisions has changed significantly in terms of needs. Many of the children who were in the special school system during the 1980s – those with moderate learning difficulties and those with physical and/or sensory disabilities – are these days, thanks to inclusive policy, educated in mainstream schools alongside their peers. However, their place in special schools has been taken by a newly emerged population, polarised in two different directions. In the late 1970s, the condition of autism was only beginning to be recognised and diagnosed. Since that time there has been a growing understanding of the condition as a spectrum of disorders, and there has been a corresponding explosion in identification and diagnosis, of autism as a discrete condition, but also as an adjunct to other difficulties/disabilities. Alongside this, the development of sophisticated neonatal medical interventions has meant that babies born pre-term, at 20 to 30 weeks, who previously would not have survived, can be kept alive, but are at risk of significant disabilities. Similarly, what were once life-limiting conditions can be more effectively treated, giving such children a longer life expectancy. This gives us a group of children with highly complex needs who, as the present education system is organised (and more on this in Chapter 1), would be unlikely to have their needs adequately met in mainstream schools.

The nature of the inclusion debate has also changed over the last thirty-five years, and the term 'inclusion' is itself contentious, having moved from meaning 'the inclusion of SEND children in mainstream provisions', to a broadening understanding of *who* should be included (any children perceived to be 'different' or from marginalised groups). Latterly, in what might be argued is the biggest circumvention of the issue, there has been debate around *where* inclusion might take place, meaning within any school community, including special schools, resulting in the oddly contradictory position that a child can be segregated whilst at the same time being included.

What has been learned more than anything since the Warnock Committee first proposed the 'integration' of children with SEND in 1978, is that the inclusion of children with additional learning needs is challenging, and for many children the inclusive educational experience remains a poor one, characterised by a lack of understanding of their needs, poor resourcing and bullying by their peers. Even Mary Warnock, one of the chief proponents of the concept of inclusion recognised, in 2005, that it was failing many children. So why might this be? In the wider context, inclusion does not sit easily with educational policies that focus on attainment and achievement, and it tests the creativity of practitioners to the limit. At the same time, in teacher training the amount of time devoted to the inclusion of children with SEND has dwindled, meaning that NQTs are often ill-prepared and lacking in confidence. As the industrialisation and mass production values of the late nineteenth century led to the social exclusion of disabled adults, so the mass education system militates against children and young people who 'can't keep up'. Certainly, practitioners on the front line attempting to implement inclusive policy in schools, struggle on a daily basis to include children who may be 'different'. So why do we persevere? The reason we include is simple and boils down to rights, entitlements and life chances; ensuring that all children have the same opportunities to succeed. Segregating children into separate education limits their chances and perpetuates attitudes of suspicion, fear and pity around disability.

The early years, however, provide a unique opportunity for making inclusion a success, as this is where inclusion is at its most straightforward. Since the mid-1990s there has been a renewed focus on early childhood education and care. Recognition of its value has led to an increase in the numbers of settings and the number of children at various ages who access it. In 2013, there were 17,900 full daycare settings, and 7,100 sessional providers. School-based provision was made up of 400 nursery schools, and 7,600 primary schools also had nursery classes. There has been a continuous move away from sessional care and towards full day provision, which has been supported in part by increased government funding. This suggests, not surprisingly, an ongoing change in the nature of care that is needed by parents (DfE 2013). In effect, the majority of 3- and 4-year-olds, 40 per cent of 2-year-olds, and many younger children, now attend some form of early years provision. From September 2014, 2-year-olds for whom Disability Living Allowance is paid, also became entitled to free early education (DfE 2015), and the Special Educational Needs and Disabilities Code of Practice and the Early Years Foundation Stage guidance (DfE 2014a) also require that all those working with young children are alert to emerging difficulties and respond to these early. Early years settings will therefore support a proportion of children already diagnosed with SEND, alongside those who will have a need identified whilst in the provision. According to the Early Years Foundation Stage framework, all Ofsted-registered early years providers, and schools offering early years provision, must ensure that children learn and develop well and are kept healthy and safe. As part of this requirement, settings must have arrangements in place that include a clear strategy for assessing SEND, as part of the overall approach to monitoring the progress and development of all children (DfE 2014a). Maintained nursery schools and other providers who are funded by the local authority to deliver early education places must have regard to the special educational needs (SEND) Code of Practice (DfE 2015).

Practitioners in early years settings, in my experience, have the freedom, and the skills and the imagination, to respond to a wide range of learning styles. Principles of learning through play (however that may look) and starting from the child are well established. The early years are a time when there remains (at present) some flexibility with the curriculum. This is also the time when children with additional needs are likely to be closest, developmentally, to their peers. White et al. (2010) also note that joint provision and coordination between SEN services, health and social care is better established within early years provision. It is a time when the foundations can be laid for both disabled and non-disabled children's experiences of inclusive education and for parents' confidence in the staff in inclusive settings to understand and meet the needs of their child. In addition to having the tools needed to offer practical support to children with SEND and their parents/carers, this is also an opportunity to work with young children and their carers to lay down some of the attitudes and values that will remain with them throughout their lives. The question in early years settings is not 'should we include?' but 'how can we include?' This is the crucial age/stage at which many children with SEND are identified and at which prompt intervention is vital. Frequently, the perceived barrier to inclusion is a lack of resources. But my experience is that the most important factor is practitioner confidence. Early years teachers and practitioners often lack the confidence to effectively support disabled children and their families. Much is demanded of practitioners in the early years. They are expected to be ever more creative with their approach, but often lack the training and experience to do this effectively. And flexibility is fast becoming eroded by the push towards 'school readiness', which brings with it increasing pressures to formalise early years education and offer an increasingly restricted early years curriculum.

This is a book written by practitioners (or former practitioners) to support current and prospective early years practitioners to meet some of the challenges of implementing inclusive practice in early years settings.

PART

I

Principles of inclusion

Why include children with SEND?

Chris Collett

This chapter looks at:

- inclusion as a contested concept

- the origins and development of inclusive practice

- changing attitudes to disability, from negative historical stereotypes of fear, suspicion and pity to present-day understanding

- the influence of key models of disability; medical and social

- the moral argument for inclusion in the context of rights and opportunities

- current barriers to inclusion

One of the most powerful barriers to the equal participation of children with SEND, is not the inevitable result of their impairments or medical conditions, but the prejudicial attitudes of others. During the course of a career spanning thirty-five years, I have come into contact with many early years practitioners and teachers, as well as students, who were keen to include. But I often found that whilst inclusion was accepted on principle as being a 'good thing', there was often little understanding of *why* this is so. As will be discussed later in this chapter, including children with SEND can present challenges and if there isn't a strong rationale on which it's based, then it is all too easy to think that it is unimportant and to give up on it when the going gets tough. Practitioners not only need to be confident to address the needs of the disabled child, but also, at a time when there may be anxieties about children's progress, they need to be able to articulate to colleagues and sometimes to parents, the reasoning behind the inclusion of a child who may be perceived as 'difficult' and demanding of practitioners' time and resources.

Where a child's disability is evident, as in the case, for example, of cerebral palsy, this may be more straightforward, but it is less so where a child has a 'hidden' disability, such as autism spectrum disorder (ASD). Although there has undoubtedly been a shift in thinking about disability that moves away from historic stereotypes, the default position remains, in education, that disability presents a potential issue or problem. In the wider world, there has, in recent years, been a resurgence of negativity in the media rhetoric around disabled people as 'benefit scroungers' and, according to Coleman, Sykes and Walker (2013), 39,000 adults per year, in the period 2009–12, were the victims of disability hate crime. This reflex comes as a direct result of centuries of suspicion, fear and pity surrounding disabled people, and, in order to fully understand why these attitudes remain so deeply embedded in the public consciousness, it is necessary to explore where they originated.

A history of segregation

Ancient history tells a grim story of the treatment of disabled children. The ancient Greeks and Romans regarded imperfection and deformity as abominations, and any such affliction as a judgement from their gods (Reiser in Cole 2012; Brignall 2008). The lives of disabled people were considered of little value, except for the purposes of entertainment, and Quarmby (2011:24) records that 'dwarves, hunchbacks and fools' were much in demand amongst the wealthy, for this purpose. Many malformed or disabled infants were discreetly disposed of, before their births could be registered, a practice that was positively encouraged. Disabled children who did survive to live into adulthood were perceived as being a burden on society, as their economic contribution was limited, and they were shunned by the wider population (Quarmby 2011).

The perception of disability as a 'punishment' for wrongdoing that carried with it a shameful stigma, was reinforced by the major organised religions, which established the importance of so-called 'miracle cures'. This added to the belief that disability, by definition, was undesirable and unacceptable (Reiser in Cole 2012). Where tolerance towards disabled individuals did exist, within isolated rural communities, disabled people were nonetheless consigned to the lowest ranks of society, a status that has ever since been a guiding factor in the framing of social policy, with disabled people often considered only as an afterthought.

During the middle ages, the suspicion surrounding disability was further strengthened through witch hunts that were, in effect, nothing more than the persecution of women who might be perceived as different due to a physical deformity or eccentric behaviour (Quarmby 2011). These women became the scapegoats for any ill fortune, a theme that persists through folklore, with the portrayal of wicked witches and evil goblins in fairy tales (Reiser in Cole 2012).

Reflective activity

Think about the characters in fairy stories you were read as a child.
   Were there particular characteristics that helped you to recognise the villain?
   How many of these were physical imperfections?

The exploitation of disabled people as 'entertainment' saw a resurgence in Victorian England through freak shows and country fairs, and this pastime was later extended, making 'lunatic asylums' accessible to the viewing public, the most famous of which was Bedlam (Quarmby 2011). But whilst all of these practices helped to firmly establish damaging perceptions of disability, the biggest upheaval in the lives of disabled people was yet to come.

The industrial revolution of the nineteenth century triggered a mass migration of people from rural communities to the factories of the industrial towns and cities. Due to their impairments, many disabled people were unable to meet the demands of mass production, where tasks often required dexterity or physical strength and had to be carried out quickly and to rigorous standards. Doctors began to identify those who were unsuitable for such work, consigning them instead to the filthy, infested poorhouses or workhouses, at the same time separating them from the rest of the population. Unable to fulfil a paid role, disabled people were at the mercy of handouts from the state, and diagnosis and categorisation suddenly became the key to accessing what meagre resources were available (Reiser in Cole 2012; Borsay 2006). Help from charitable organisations only helped to reinforce ideas of disabled people as pitiable and dependent on others (Harris and Roulstone 2012).

Mike Oliver's medical model framework helps to describe perceptions at that time and through to the middle part of the twentieth century (Figure 1.1).

Reflective activity

Consider the main features of the medical model of disability. To what extent do these ideas continue to resonate today?

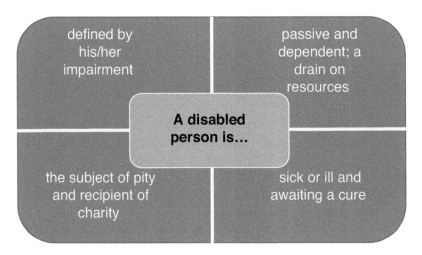

Figure 1.1 The medical model. Adapted from Oliver (1990)

The wholesale removal of disabled people from mainstream society helped to fuel the fear and superstition that surrounded them, and such attitudes were given further weight by the growth towards the end of the nineteenth century of social Darwinism and the emergence of the eugenics movement (Hodkinson and Vickerman 2009). A movement supported by influential figures, such as Francis Galton and Winston Churchill, eugenics saw disabled people as weak, and a threat to the future of humankind. These ideas led to the further incarceration of thousands of disabled people to prevent them from procreating, and distinctions between the disabled, the degenerate and the criminal became blurred. The policy was taken to its extreme in Nazi Germany, when tens of thousands of disabled people were killed in the Holocaust, during the Second World War.

Reflective activity

Think about the children who were segregated from their families at a very young age.

What effects would this have had on them and their families?

How would this practice fit with our current understanding of attachment?

Changing perceptions

So what effect did all this thinking have on the education of disabled children? It was felt for a long time that children with disabilities, especially physical and learning disabilities, could not benefit from education. Before 1944, the only specialist educational provision in England was a handful of schools set up by charities or church organisations, primarily for deaf or blind children. Children with less clearly definable disabilities remained in the asylums (later to become mental handicap hospitals), often due to what would today be considered relatively minor conditions, such as epilepsy. Life in such institutions was harsh; children were frequently subjected to cruel, experimental medical 'treatments' and were at risk of abuse (Borsay 2006). It wasn't until the mid-twentieth century that things began to change, in response to the growing understanding of equality and human rights.

Following the atrocities of the Second World War, the 1948 UN Declaration of Human Rights proclaimed that 'All human beings are born free and equal in dignity and rights', and introduced principles of equal opportunities, dignity, self-determination and non-discrimination, for the protection of vulnerable minority groups. Originating in the US, during the 1950s and early '60s the disability rights movement began to take hold in Britain. This marked the beginning of a coordinated approach to tackling the injustices to which disabled people had been and were being subjected. Traditional ideas were challenged and increasingly disability was viewed as a form of social oppression (Hodkinson and Vickerman 2009).

With this movement came the growing recognition that disabled people were being denied educational opportunities and, as a result, the chance to participate fully in society (Quarmby 2011). In response, the 1970 Education (Handicapped Children) Act deemed that *all* children had a legal entitlement to a 'full and broad' education, bringing all children, even those with the most complex needs, from health care services into the remit of local education authorities (Hodkinson and Vickerman 2009). However, for many children with disabilities, this meant within a segregated (separate) system of special education, so that their presence would not 'inconvenience the smooth running of normal schools' (Fredrickson and Cline 2002). These special schools, usually catering for specific categories of disability, were few and far between, and often meant that children had to travel long distances and could be forced to board from an early age and against the wishes of their parents. Borsay (in Haines and Ruebain 2010) highlights the isolating effects and the long-term damage of these practices, which were compounded by low expectations, few opportunities for academic qualifications and consequently poor employment opportunities, leading to a lifetime of dependency. The rights of children with disabilities, and even their parents in choosing provision, were still not keeping pace with concepts of rights and equality.

Disabled rights activists, many of whom had been disadvantaged by special schools, continued to press for a change to oppressive medical

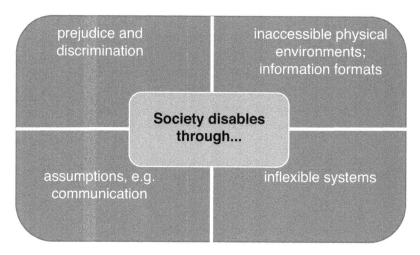

Figure 1.2 The social model. Adapted from Oliver (1990)

model thinking, and a new way of framing disability began to emerge. The social model of disability recognises that an individual is disabled, not by his or her impairment, but by the environment in which he or she lives, works or is educated (Figure 1.2).

As well as other aspects of daily life, this changing understanding was reflected in changes occurring in educational provision, and so began, in the 1970s and 80s, a move to reverse the policy of segregation for disabled children. Progress was formalised by the Warnock Report (1978), which paved the way for their 'integration' into mainstream schools. The 1974 committee chaired by Mary Warnock heralded a move away from medically imposed categories of disability, instead proposing an all-embracing term *special educational needs*. This also shifted the emphasis away from individual deficits (what was 'wrong' with the child) to what provision was needed to support his or her learning. Any additional resources that were required would be accessed through an individual 'statement of need' (Hodkinson and Vickerman 2009; Fredrickson and Cline 2002). The Warnock committee also saw the importance of early identification of needs and speedy interventions, the creation of effective partnerships with parents and the need to take a coordinated multi-agency approach (DES 1978).

The Warnock Report was to set the blueprint for the education of children with SEND for decades to come and key recommendations were enforced through the 1981 Education Act. From that point on 'integration' and later 'inclusion' into mainstream schools became the central plank of education policy for children with SEND. And whilst the concept of inclusion has been an evolving one, its purpose remains to ensure that disabled children have the same opportunities in education, employment and life, as their peers.

Implementing inclusion

To make inclusion a reality, successive governments since Warnock (1978) have pursued policies to close segregated special schools in favour of an inclusive education system. These policies have been underpinned by further disability legislation, the most influential of which has been the Special Needs and Disability Act (SENDA, 2001; derived from the 1995 Disability Discrimination Act) which makes it unlawful for mainstream schools and settings to exclude children with SEND without legal justification (Fredrickson and Cline 2002; Hodkinson and Vickerman 2009). Increasingly, at the policy level, the approach has followed the social model of disability and 'integration' has given way to 'inclusion' which requires a whole school approach, ensuring that the needs of a wide range of children are met.

But the gap between the ideal and what happens in practice is often a big one and since the late 1990s there has been growing anecdotal evidence that many children with SEND have been poorly served by the policy of inclusion. In 2005, Mary Warnock cited what she called the 'disastrous legacy' of her 1978 report, and highlighted 'limits to what can be achieved in mainstream schools, given the diversity of children's needs and the finite available resources' (Warnock in Cigman 2007:xii). Soon after, the Lamb Inquiry (DCSF 2009) observed that 'while the aims of the SEN framework remain relevant, implementation has often failed to live up to them', leaving children with SEND educationally vulnerable.

This has not been helped by the increased confusion about what exactly we mean by 'inclusion'. In the 1970s and 1980s, the concept

Reflective activity

1. *Inclusion is founded upon a moral position which values and respects every individual and which welcomes diversity as a rich learning resource. It means the restructuring of mainstream provision so that all schools are willing and able to include, value and respect all children.*
(Centre for Studies in Inclusive Education 2013)

2. *In the northern hemisphere [inclusion] has become about trying to break down segregated systems, whilst in the south the priority is ensuring the inclusion of all marginalized groups in some form of basic education.*
(UNESCO 2003)

3. *Inclusion involves having an education service that ensures that provision and funding is there to enable pupils to be educated in the most appropriate setting.*
(National Association of Head Teachers 2003)

Look at the definitions of inclusion. How do they reflect the ethos of the organisations represented?

of inclusion was interpreted in the UK as meaning full inclusion into mainstream provision for children with SEND. However, with the 1990s school improvement agenda, inclusion became more about attempts to improve the educational outcomes for *all* children, including those who were socially and economically disadvantaged (Hodkinson and Vickerman 2009), and the waters became muddied.

So, what is it about inclusion that 'hasn't worked'?

There are a number of tensions in the system of inclusion as it has evolved. One of these has been a model that links funding directly to the individual child's identified needs; so, the greater the need, the greater the resources required to meet those needs. This inevitably means highlighting the child's 'deficits', that is, what s/he is *unable* to do, which goes against the ethos of the rights-based social model of disability. The Warnock Report recommendation of having a single category of 'special educational needs' attempted to move away from this labelling, and yet the process of meeting those needs positively encourages it. In 2005, Mary Warnock herself also identified what she felt to be a flaw in the term 'special educational needs', which implies that children with SEND belong to one homogenous group, with the same or similar characteristics, when in reality their differences are many and varied. And it is arguable whether it is possible to provide effectively for learners' differences without singling them out as different.

From 2001, education settings, both state maintained and non-maintained, have been legally required to identify, assess and provide for children with SEN through procedures set out in the 2001 SEN Code of Practice (DfES 2001a). Local authorities both determine those needs and take responsibility for meeting them within a defined budget. While this funding arrangement has long been viewed as a conflict of interests, and a 2006 House of Commons Select Committee went as far as making recommendations for change (Audit Commission 2007), this is yet to be implemented. A lack of clear, tight criteria for funding has also meant that although schools and LEAs may follow the procedures rigorously, their interpretations of them might differ widely, and so there has been a lack of equity in meeting the needs of children, both within and across local authorities. The balancing act between budgets and children's needs, especially as the financial year progresses, has often left schools and settings with insufficient funding to meet educational and care needs, and therefore has left children vulnerable to educational failure and bullying. The battle for funding has made the statementing process adversarial and open to abuse. Frequently, those parents who are the most articulate and assertive have their child's needs met (Warnock and Norwich 2010), while children who do not have the benefit of strong advocates, are at a disadvantage. Notably, the children and young people who lose out the most are children with SEND from minority ethnic groups, or who are looked after by the state.

A further tension has arisen from the conflict between the inclusion agenda and the drive to raise standards and create competition between schools that began with the introduction of the National Curriculum in 1988. Rogers (2007) found that many children supposedly 'included' in mainstream, were, in practice, excluded in different ways: either removed from the group for individual support, unable to access material presented to them or unable to form meaningful relationships with their peers. This, she argues, is made worse by a continuing lack of knowledge and understanding about difference, but also by the stringent 'testing and examination' structure in our schools. In addition, the caveat that has traditionally accompanied inclusive policy – that it is viable only if it does not compromise the education of non-disabled children – means that many SEND children, chiefly those with emotional and behavioural difficulties, are subject to short- or long-term exclusion and left at the mercy of overstretched and inconsistent support services.

Outcomes for children and young people

The real test of the success of inclusive policy should be whether or not it has made a difference to the lives of children and young people with SEND in terms of better outcomes. But, despite the fact that policy has been driven in this direction for almost forty years, there is surprisingly little in the way of systematic evaluation or evidence of impact. Most studies that have been conducted are on a small scale and based to a large extent on evidence from the US. The assessment of outcomes can be problematic, given the diverse and fluctuating population of children with SEND, and many outcomes are described in subjective terms that are not easily definable. Research in England at the start of the twenty-first century attempted to assess the broader impact of inclusion, by looking at schools' academic results, but little or no correlation was found and it was felt that other factors, such as poverty and social deprivation, may have had a more significant influence over outcomes than disability and inclusion (Farrell et al. 2007).

Ofsted (2006) found that the best outcomes for pupils with learning difficulties and disabilities (LDD) were determined not by the type of provision, but by the quality. The most important factors contributing to good progress were: 'the involvement of a specialist teacher; good assessment; work tailored to challenge pupils sufficiently; and commitment from school leaders to ensure good progress for all pupils', all of which it could be said are more likely to occur in specialist provisions (Ofsted 2006:6). Additionally, the report found that children with emotional behavioural difficulties (EBD) were least likely to receive effective support, or received it too late. However, underlying the report is an acknowledged lack of agreement regarding what 'good progress' for pupils with LDD actually means.

Perhaps not surprisingly, given the range of additional variables that would need to be considered, there appears to have been little investigation into the experiences of individual children with SEND regarding their future life opportunities, although Russell (2008) found that children with disabilities are still twice as likely as their non-disabled peers to leave school with no formal qualifications. Aiming High for Disabled Children, which emerged from the Every Disabled Child Matters (EDCM) campaign in the mid 2000s, noted that 17 per cent of disabled young people were not in education, employment or training, compared with only 7 per cent of non-disabled young people; disabled children were over eight times more likely to be excluded from school than their non-disabled peers and that 80 per cent of disabled children had been bullied compared with fewer than two thirds of their peers (DfES and HM Treasury 2007). There is scant evidence to suggest that this has changed in the interim.

Central to the concept of inclusion is the sense of 'belonging', something that Warnock (2005:15) argues 'appears to be necessary both for successful learning and for more general wellbeing'. A number of studies in the 1990s found that there were positive effects of inclusion for children with SEND in terms of social skills, self-concept and a 'reduced fear of differences', which would seem to meet one of the goals of inclusion in terms of helping to change attitudes (Kalambouka et al. 2007:367). But findings have not been wholly positive. Using a range of measures, including 'belonging' scales, Frederickson et al. (2007:109) looked at one particular inclusion project in the UK and found that whilst former special school children were positively accepted by their peers, children with SEND already placed in mainstream provision were not, which might simply indicate that particular efforts were made by staff to assimilate the children transferring from special schools. Peer attitude research, conducted chiefly in the US, further indicates that children with SEND who are included experience higher levels of social rejection, bullying and victimisation, and are less accepted than their mainstream peers.

Special schools have historically been criticised for their low expectations, and the Lamb Inquiry (2009) found that this was not necessarily different for children with SEND included in mainstream provisions. The Achievement for All Strategy (AfA; National College 2010) marked efforts to raise expectations and achievements in the broadest sense for all children, including those with SEND. It recognised the indirect impact on attainment of the raised self-esteem and confidence that arise from success in a range of out of school activities, and attempted to address the fact that children with SEND have traditionally been exposed to fewer opportunities for these activities. AfA took a rights-based collaborative approach and reported significant improvements in relationships, pupil behaviour and attendance, along with a reduction in numbers of children identified with SEND within the schools that espoused the initiative (Ekins 2012). However, despite the positive outcomes reported, it is interesting to note that rather than being adopted as a mainstream strategy, which would suggest a level of entitlement, AfA subsequently went on to acquire charitable status, taking it outside the mainstream and signalling a return to the reliance on 'goodwill' for meeting the needs of disabled children and young people.

Why has inclusion foundered?

There are a number of reasons why, in schools at least, inclusion seems to have stalled. Some would argue, Armstrong et al. (2010) among them, that the problem is that inclusive policy has not gone far enough. All that has been tried so far, is to fit children into an existing system, instead of taking the more radical step of redesigning the system to be an inclusive one. Barton (2005:5) suggests that this is because of a 'lack of political will' on the part of governments, and indeed it would be a brave politician who would propose the costly and disruptive restructuring of England's education system that would be required.

Critics of 'full inclusion' for children with SEND, would assert that it overlooks the obvious practical realities of disability and the rights of other children to an effective education (Hodkinson and Vickerman 2009:80). This has led to the growing belief, in this country, that inclusion is not about location, but about choice, and about access to a high-quality education that leads to equal opportunities in later life. It places special schools within the definition of inclusion as part of a spectrum of provision (Tutt 2007). Tutt goes on to assert that the increased cooperation between mainstream and specialist schools in England has created a 'flexible continuum of provision', in which all children are included within the wider community of the school. However, this acceptance of continuing segregation is directly at odds with the United Nations Convention on the Rights of Persons with Disabilities (UNCRPD) which states that 'children with disabilities should have full enjoyment of all human rights and fundamental freedoms *on an equal basis with other children* [my emphasis]' (UN 2006), and specifically with Article 24 that calls for children with disabilities *not* to be excluded from the general education system. And whilst the UK has ratified the convention, it is with the caveat of 'the right for disabled children to be educated outside their local community where more appropriate education provision is available elsewhere' (Disability Action 2016).

So, on the one hand we have the rhetoric of inclusive education as a fundamental human right, but on the other, despite ideological commitment, is a clear ambivalence, both at practitioner level, where barriers to inclusion would appear to focus on lack of resources and continuing negative attitudes, and also at the wider policy level, both of which deny the right to participation of children with SEND leaving them vulnerable to limited opportunities in later life. Perhaps surprisingly, the parents' lobby against inclusion has also been a powerful one. Organisations such as the Gloucestershire Special Schools Protection League (Telegraph 2005) were instrumental in keeping special schools open. Batten et al. (2006), in their report *Make School Make Sense. Autism and education: the reality for families today*, found that parents were in favour of a range of provision including mainstream schools, special schools, resource bases in mainstream schools and dual placements. Over 40 per cent of children with autism surveyed had experienced bullying at school, with one in five children being excluded and 67 per cent of those excluded more than once. Additionally, groups such as those with sensory impairments (blind, deaf and deafblind), see inclusive education as a denial of the individualised support they need, and actively campaign to retain the opportunity for segregated learning. The Green Paper 'Support and aspiration', which preceded the 2014 Children and Families Act, even went as far as the recommendation to 'remove the bias towards inclusion', though this did not go on to appear in the final legislation.

Concerns about the flaws in the existing system of inclusion prompted a flurry of reviews of SEND provision, including the House of Commons Report (2006), The Bercow Report (2008) and the Lamb Inquiry (2009) along with 'Support and Aspiration'. From these, a number of issues were identified:

- parent confidence (in the system);

- parent involvement and control;

- early identification and categorisation of SEND;

- a complex and unwieldy statutory assessment process, in which ultimate responsibility (regardless of need), fell to schools and education settings;

- a need for more effective collaboration between services, including the voluntary and community sectors;

- conflicts of interest in statutory provision and funding.

The future of inclusion

What emerged from this melting pot were the Children and Families Act 2014 and the SEND Code of Practice 2015, published jointly by the Department of Health and Department for Education. It is interesting to consider what, in these, has changed. Replacing statements of SEN with negotiated education, health and care (EHC) plans will undoubtedly encourage more strategic collaborative working across the main sectors, and spread the responsibility for funding more evenly – in fact, colleagues working in the field report anecdotally that this is already happening. That EHCs and the preceding personalised learning plans are to be 'outcomes focused' also attempts to place the child, rather than the available resources, at the centre of the process. The introduction of optional personal budgets will allow for some parents to have more control, and the requirement for local authorities to publish a comprehensive 'Local Offer' of available services across education, health, social care and community introduces a new degree of transparency and will highlight gaps in provision.

However, it could still be argued that these are simply further adjustments to the existing system and that some things remain resolutely the same. The criteria for inclusion in mainstream are reasonably enough subject to the needs of the child. But the criteria of 'efficient use of resources' and the disruption of education of non-disabled children, still leave scope for settings who do not wish to include to make their case. And the new legislation has not been published at a happy time for services to children and families. Newly formed free schools and academies, whilst required to meet the same obligations as maintained schools with regards to SEND legislation, will nonetheless, over time, encourage a more selective and segregationist approach. And the proposals for new grammar schools, should it go ahead, would only compound this.

Conclusion

Progress in inclusion has been made, but SEND continues to often be viewed as a problem. The key to changing this stance is to change attitudes and this can be started with young children through the overt acceptance of difference, disability awareness and positive practitioner attitudes. Resources too can help promote inclusive attitudes to disability (see Chapter 5). And what of the wider impact of inclusive education on participation, equal opportunities, dignity and self-determination for children and young people with disabilities? According to the Centre for Studies in Inclusive Education (CSIE) the route to an inclusive society is through an inclusive education system that helps create a society in which disabled children, young people and adults can enjoy the same rights, freedoms and opportunities as anyone else and have the same chances of experiencing success in later life. After thirty years of inclusive policy, how far can we say that has been achieved?

Further reading

Hodkinson, A (2015) *Key Issues in Special Educational Needs and Inclusion.* London: Sage.

Quarmby, K (2011) *Scapegoat: why we are failing disabled people.* London: Portobello Books.

Ekins, A (2012) *The Changing Face of Special Educational Needs.* Abingdon: Routledge.

Assessment, early identification and individualised learning

2

Sue Mitchell and Karen Thorpe

This chapter looks at:

- the role of observation, assessment and information gathering in identifying SEND
- the current statutory framework for assessment and identification, including the EYFS, the SEND Code of Practice and the 2-year health check
- early intervention through the assess, plan, do and review cycle
- differentiation, task analysis and teaching strategies
- outcomes-focused record keeping through the one page profile
- requesting and contributing to the EHC

The UK has a long tradition of providing education and childcare for babies and pre-school children. However, this provision received little government attention, investment and regulation prior to the last twenty years. Since 2001, all early years settings have had to have regard to the SEN Code of Practice 2001. This code required each setting to have a named Special Education Needs Co-ordinator (SENCo) and placed a duty on all practitioners to play a part in both identifying and meeting the needs of children with special educational needs (SEN). From 2008, the Early Years Foundation Stage (EYFS) set out the principle of the 'unique child' which supported the philosophy of inclusion by recognising that children develop and learn in different ways and at different rates, thus requiring a unique response from their educators. The early years practitioner was therefore required to observe and assess in order to create a picture of each child's interests, learning style and level of achievement. This knowledge was to inform the planning of individualised learning experiences. The current statutory framework (DfE 2014a) embeds equality of opportunity and anti-discriminatory practice as a key principle, to ensure that every child is included and supported.

The current EYFS guidance became effective in September 2014, alongside the current SEND Code of Practice (2015) which followed the 2014 Children and Families Act. To meet the requirements of both, every early years practitioner must adopt a child- and family-centred approach and plan and implement activities and experiences which enable the child to realise individualised outcomes.

Every early years setting is required to have written policies which reflect its inclusive ethos and detail how it identifies, assesses and meets individual needs. They should include reference to how the curriculum, resources, environment and staffing are used to support the learning and development of children with SEND. In addition, policies will detail practice in relation to being responsive to the voice of the child, partnership with parents/carers and working with other agencies. The role of the setting-based SENCo remains central.

Knowing the child – building up a picture

Children arrive in early years settings with a wide range of prior experiences and may or may not have accessed previous early education. Early educators need to develop an holistic view of the unique child within the family and community context. Most settings will do this through:

Collecting background information

Early years settings will be familiar with requesting information during admission and induction processes. Admissions paperwork will collect information about ethnicity, home language, religion, address and family. It will give an opportunity for parents/carers to detail previous educational settings, medical history, health needs and other professionals involved (e.g. health visitor, social worker). Where a child starts at a setting after their second birthday, information about their 2-year health and development review with the health visitor should be requested.

Many settings make use of an 'all about me' sheet to gather information about children's preferences, significant relationships, strengths and needs, communication and personal care.

Admissions paperwork may also allow parents to summarise any concerns about their child's development or to inform practitioners of an already identified special educational need or disability.

Induction/settling in

Settings implement a range of induction procedures for the purpose of supporting the child's separation from their parent/carer. This period allows for the development of the child's relationship with their key person and key group and their awareness of the environment and routines. Many settings release staff to make home visits, enabling an understanding of the family environment.

Initial observation

Early years practitioners will need to be skilled at making observations to support a growing knowledge of each child. This will include both non-participant observation (watching and listening) and participant observation (noting the child's responses while directly interacting with them). These routine observations can alert staff to possible areas of delay, which would then need more detailed observations to either confirm or allay concerns.

Baseline assessment

This will be a summative assessment of the child's learning and development against the early years outcomes. Whilst this needs to be carried
out soon after entry to a setting, there does need to be consideration
of the child's emotional well-being, as children can take time to settle
and to present typically when in any new situation. Staff should seek
to wait until the child is relaxed, comfortable and understands what is
expected. Baseline assessments will confirm current levels of development in the EYFS prime and specific areas and indicate whether or not
the child is achieving age appropriate outcomes.

Any of the above may:

- alert staff to a need/disability which has yet to be formally identified;

- inform staff of how an identified special educational need or disability impacts on the child's development.

More detailed assessment

Practitioners will need to make more detailed observations in relation
to the presenting areas of need. Initial information will guide staff as
to the most appropriate focused observations to make and the type of
format to use.

Case study 2.1: Asha

Background information

Asha is 3 years old. When she recently started at the nursery her
parents informed the staff that she is their first child and she has an
older half-sister who stays at weekends, enjoys caring for Asha and

tends to answer questions for her. Mum has previously taken Asha to a stay and play group and noticed that other children her age were using more language. She has shared this with Asha's health visitor check prior to Asha starting at the setting. There is due to be a review appointment with the health visitor next month.

During settling, staff notice that Asha tends to babble when she is playing and that her babble contains a limited range of speech sounds. She rarely approaches an adult but seems to follow instructions and the nursery routine well. She has a preference for physical and messy play and seems to enjoy the company of her peers.

Initial observation and assessment

Following a period of initial observations, staff share Asha's mother's concerns around speech and language development. Her physical development seems age appropriate and she is generally comfortable in the company of adults and peers

Focused observations

Staff carry out a series of focused observations. Staff observe Asha in a range of contexts throughout the session and keep a tally sheet which records when she speaks and how she responds to the language of others. This informs them that Asha rarely initiates communication using language but she makes some needs known using gestures such as beckoning and pointing to indicate a choice. She does however respond appropriately to almost all instructions. A tracking observation indicates that in free play she frequently chooses activities that are less dependent on spoken communication, such as physical play, construction and craft activities. A detailed observation of her interaction shows that whilst she plays alongside peers and can respond to their language in play, she is rarely understood by them and often withdraws.

Focused observations confirm that Asha has a delay in her speech and expressive language. This is impacting on her social interaction in some situations. Staff use the observations they have made to support completing an overall development assessment which indicates that all other areas of Asha's development are age appropriate. Asha has a specific delay.

* How would you use the background information and the information gained through observation and assessment to plan for Asha's next steps?

* Which professional(s) might you consider making referrals to?

Understanding developmental delay

Once a child has been identified as having a delay in their development, it is important to seek to understand why. Not every child presenting with a delay will necessarily have a special educational need or disability. A delay may be the result of one or more factors; these might include:

* family context, e.g. parenting patterns;

* social influences, e.g. poverty which limits access to stimulating environments and resources;

* environmental factors, e.g. nature of housing and geographical location;

* health issues, e.g. medical condition experienced by the child or a family member.

One or more of these factors may limit or deny a child the opportunity to develop age appropriate skills in one or more areas of development. However, in some cases, a delay in development may relate directly to a special educational need or disability (SEND) as defined in the Introduction. In seeking to understanding why a child presents with a delay in their development, quality background information is of vital importance. In settings where best practice is followed, background information is requested prior to admission and may be added to throughout induction, as the relationship with parents develops. This information should be shared with the relevant staff in the setting as it can make a significant difference to the understanding of a child's development delay. If information gained by one member of a staff team is not recorded or shared with others, there can be a delay in planning appropriately for a child.

The two brief case studies, 2.1 and 2.2, demonstrate the importance of background information.

Case study 2.2: Harry

Harry is 2 years old; he is reluctant to go outside to play and prefers to remain near to a member of staff. He has a growing vocabulary of single words and effectively makes his needs known. He accesses a range of activities with encouragement and seems to watch adults using the toys and resources before exploring them himself. He sometimes appears unsteady on his feet and tends to watch the others engaging in physical play.

- *What do you notice about Harry's development?*
- *Which areas would you focus on for further observation?*

Focused observations

Initial information raises some concerns about Harry's physical development, particularly his gross motor skills. In the other prime areas of the EYFS he generally presents as age appropriate. Staff carry out a series of focused observations of Harry engaged in physical play and movement around the setting. These confirm that Harry often holds onto furniture for support when pulling to stand. He walks with a wide gait and his steps are often uneven in size. He tends to hold his arms out when walking more quickly. He often bumps into furniture and trips over items on the floor. He does not raise one leg in an attempt to kick a ball. He is yet to control a spoon and can find it difficult to manipulate some toys. Staff agree that Harry presents with a physical development delay.

- *What further information do the focused observations give and how do these relate to what was first noticed about Harry's development?*

Background information

Harry was born at full term in hospital. After returning home to their tenth floor flat, Mum developed postnatal depression. She has a very limited support network and was ill for the first 18 months of Harry's life. She still finds it difficult to take Harry out in the community. A new health visitor has encouraged Mum to take Harry to nursery and has made a referral to family support services based at the local Children's Centre.

- *What factors may have contributed to Harry's delay in development?*
- *How could you plan to support Harry to make progress?*
- *Do you think Harry is most likely to need long- or short-term support?*

Case study 2.3: Grace

Grace is 2 years old; she waits for an adult to hold her hand whenever she moves around the setting and outside areas. She uses a range of gestures and single words to communicate although her speech is often unclear. She always uses her left hand to hold toys and seems reluctant to try two-handed. This means she is often dependent on adult support to complete a play and learning activity.

- *What do you notice about Grace's development?*
- *Which areas would you focus on for further observation?*

Focused observations

Initial information raises some concerns about Grace's fine and gross motor development; staff also share some concerns about her speech. They carry out a series of focused observations of Grace engaged in physical play and movement around the setting. These confirm that Grace is fully dependent on an adult to help her stand and walk around the setting. She has an uneven gait and her right foot seems to drag as she moves forward. Across a range of activities, staff identify that she uses her left hand and leaves her right hand by her side. When communicating by gestures she uses her left hand. Listening more closely to her speech, staff have noticed that her speech is slow and more speech sounds are missing than would be expected of a child her age.

- *What further information do the focused observations give you and how do these relate to what you first noticed about Grace's development?*

Background information

Grace was born at 32 weeks and medics think she may have been deprived of oxygen during her birth. She was in an incubator for the first six weeks of her life. She attends six-monthly check-ups with a paediatrician and was last seen when she was 18 months old. At that appointment, there were no significant concerns around her

development although she was yet to walk and showed a preference for using her left hand.

- *What factors may have resulted in Grace's delay in development?*

- *How could you plan to support Grace to make progress?*

- *Do you think Grace is most likely to need long- or short-term support?*

Harry's development delay is likely to be the consequence of external factors and not of a learning difficulty or disability. He has had a lack of opportunity for developing his gross motor skills and may have had limited stimulation and play opportunities due to his mother's mental health condition. On the other hand, Grace's developmental delay may have been the consequence of hypoxaemia. A lack of oxygen at birth can lead to a learning difficulty which becomes increasingly evident over time. She may, for example, go on to receive a diagnosis of cerebral palsy.

If a child's development is delayed as a consequence of deprivation, additional support and access to the appropriate activities can have a significant impact on a child's rate of progress and either close or remove the gap between actual and age appropriate development. If a child's development is delayed as a result of a learning difficulty or disability, staff will need to remove any barriers to learning, make reasonable adjustments where necessary and differentiate in a range of ways to ensure that the child makes progress and realises their full potential, whether or not this might be age appropriate.

Taking account of information from other professionals

Information from 2-year check (where applicable)

In addition to the assessments carried out within the setting, staff should take account of any assessments carried out by other agencies. Every child has access to development checks carried out by their health visitor. Where historically these checks were carried out in isolation, often in clinics or children's homes, there is a national drive for this to become an integrated review implemented by both early years and health teams whenever a child attends an early education setting.

The Early Years Foundation Stage progress check at age 2 (delivered by practitioners in the early years setting) is being brought together with the healthy child programme (HCP) 2–2½ years health and development review (delivered by health visiting teams), into an integrated review. Integrating health and education reviews at this age gives a more complete picture of the child through drawing together the detailed knowledge of how the child is learning and developing day-to-day at their educational setting with the expertise of the child's health visitor at the health review along with parents' views and any concerns about their child's progress.

This combination offers the potential:

- to facilitate multi-agency working which will provide clearer and more consistent information for parents;

- to identify the child's strengths and needs in order to plan for the child's next steps towards positive outcomes in health and well-being, learning and development;

- for earlier identification and facilitation of appropriate intervention, especially for those for whom progress is less than expected;

- for earlier referrals and access to relevant support;

- to generate feedback which can be used at a strategic level to plan services and contribute to the reduction of inequalities in children's outcomes.

There may also be a need to refer children to other professionals who are qualified to confirm that a child has a developmental delay and who have the remit to identify causal factors (see Chapter 4).

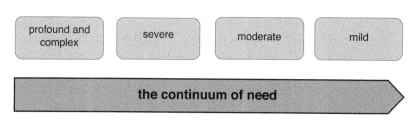

Figure 2.1 The continuum of need

Implementing the graduated approach of the 2015 SEND Code of Practice

The SEND Code of Practice 2015 outlines a 'graduated approach' to meeting special educational needs. This approach is based on the concept of a continuum of need (Figure 2.1). Children may move along this continuum, but not necessarily in only one direction. Nor will all children go on to have the highest level of need.

The graduated approach is supported by a four-part assess, plan, do, review cycle, which will already be familiar to practitioners implementing the EYFS. All early years practitioners will potentially play a role in assessing a child's current development, planning for their next steps, implementing the plan and reviewing its impact. Where there is reason to believe that a child may have, or when a child has identified SEND, the setting SENCo will also play an increasingly significant role in the cycle.

Differentiation

'High quality teaching, differentiated for individual pupils, is the first step in responding to pupils who have or may have SEN' (DfE 2015 6:37). It is important to recognise that not every underachieving child will have a special educational need. Effective differentiation may go a long way in remediating a delay in learning and development. This

will particularly be the case where children who have lacked access to appropriate play and learning experiences are given additional opportunities and support to make progress. Planning for children must be based on the stage of their current development and not their age.

Differentiation will be taking place throughout the day to respond to the individual needs of each unique child. For some children, this will need to be more structured and regular to meet the needs identified through information gathering and building a picture of the child.

Table 2.1 Methods of differentiation

Outcome – all are successful	• Different work/amounts of work produced for same activity • Different targets for the same activity
Interest – use of child's interests in an activity	• Flexibility in following child's interests during an activity • Use of interests in reward systems
Teaching style – the way in which the activity is delivered in response to a child's learning style	• Spoken – so that the child learns by listening • Visually – so that the child learns by looking • Actively – so that the child learns by moving and doing
Task	• Use of verbal and visual supports • Presentation of tasks, e.g. activity broken into small steps • Support/extension and reinforcement activities
Pace/time	• Time allowed to process information and language • Time allowed to complete an activity
Support	• Use of adult/peer support • Use of verbal and visual prompts in activities
Resources	• Use of different resources in activities • Access to resources and use of specialist resource

Recording	• Use of different ways for child and practitioners to record, e.g. verbal, written, pictures, photos, ICT, video
Organisation	• Physical layout of learning environment • Individual/paired/group or whole setting activities
Language/communication	• Complexity, level and length • Use of visual and verbal • Use of augmentative and alternative communication
Differentiation can be made in many ways, including:	• Indoor and outdoor activities • Child- or adult-led activities

Increased differentiation is that which is planned, recorded, implemented, monitored and reviewed above the routine differentiation in place in any setting. Many settings make use of a 'one-page profile' to incorporate a record of the increased differentiation in place to support a child. This profile is referred to in the 2015 SEND Code of Practice as part of the personalised agenda. One-page profiles are person-centred and capture significant information about a child. Whilst the philosophy behind these profiles is that they should be developed by the person they relate to, where very young children are concerned, their voice will often be facilitated by their parents. Since most early years practitioners are familiar with All About Me sheets, the-one page profile is not a new concept. However, thought must be given to the format of the profile if it is to be effective as a tool for addressing additional needs. All one-page profiles contain the same elements and an example is provided (Figure 2.2).

Where the one-page profile is updated over time it can create an accurate story of the child's journey and progress over time and is then extremely useful to support the education, health and care (EHC) pathway discussed later in this chapter.

My name is:		Profile Number:	Date:
Photo	What people like about me and what I can do well:		
My story:			
What's important to me now and in the future:		My parents' /carers' hopes and aspirations for me now and in the future:	
How to support meeting my needs:			
How to communicate with me:			
I like or prefer:		I don't like:	
These are some of the important people in my life:		Other things to know about me	

Figure 2.2 The one-page profile

Case study 2.4: Koby

Background information

Koby was very recently 4 years old. He is newly arrived in UK and parents have shared that he did not attend nursery provision in his birth country. He has an older sibling who he is very close to. English is the home language.

Settling and initial observations

It took longer than might typically be expected for Koby to separate from his mother without crying, and he continues to need the support of his key person on arrival to remain calm. His key person is the only member of staff to hear him speak. He carries a comfort toy at all times. He waits for his key person to support him with personal care and at meal times. He will sometimes join the group at carpet time and follows some routines when supported by an adult. He tends to stay close to his key person throughout sessions and is unlikely to engage in activities without her support. He joins in when she directs his play and tends to remain with that toy until prompted by an adult to access other activities.

Initial observation and assessment

Initial observations suggest delay in all areas of development. Staff have observed that Koby tends to play alongside rather than with peers and that he is dependent on adult support to sustain concentration on play and learning activities.

Focused observations

Staff decided to carry out focused observations within each of the prime areas. Language observations in a range of contexts indicate that Koby uses mostly single words and a few two-word phrases in preferred free play activities and single words in response to direct questions. When individual instructions are given, he responds to one or two key words and in group instructions he tends to copy the child closest to him. Observations of Koby engaged in physical activity inform staff that he waits for an adult to hold his hand on large apparatus. When joining in with ball games he runs unsteadily around chasing peers rather than making contact with the ball. Koby uses a spoon to feed himself and tends to spill food and drink each meal time. He has regular toileting accidents and is yet to remove clothing independently. Observation of focused activities shows that Koby generally sustains concentration for around 2 minutes. He is yet to show any knowledge of colour/shape/number/letter sounds. He uses a palmar grip to manipulate toys and tools. Koby enjoys all kinds of sensory play activities such as sand and water, and light and sound toys. Focused observations confirm that Koby has a global developmental delay, he is functioning at around a 2-year-old level in all areas.

Discussion with parents

The setting SENCo reviews the admissions paperwork with Koby's parents. Having developed a relationship with staff they share more than they did when he first started. They inform staff that they are very concerned about his development and had been referred for a specialist assessment in their home country. His older brother attended a special school in their home country but they feel Koby is making better progress than their older son did at the same age. They are keen for Koby to have the opportunity to go to a mainstream school with support and want him to make friends and become more independent.

* *Consider how the information above could be recorded onto the one-page profile format provided.*

SEN support

After a period of differentiation, if a child's progress is less than expected, the Code of Practice advises that 'SEN support' should be provided. In consultation with parents, the SENCo and practitioners should agree:

- the outcomes for the child;

- the expected impact on progress, development and/or behaviour;

- the interventions and support to be put into place to meet the outcomes;

- a review date.

Outcomes

Table 2.2 Outcomes

An outcome is . . .	An outcome is *not* . . .
• child-centred • the result or consequence of a period of SEN support • a description of what the child will be consistently doing following the period of intervention. It should be recorded using the child's name, e.g. 'Sam will . . .' • clearly achievable with a defined endpoint	A description of provision, such as: • what the practitioners are doing, e.g. 'encouraging', 'supporting', 'providing' • the resources provided • the activities and strategies delivered • a description of progress and consolidation and should not include words such as 'to develop', 'to improve', 'to increase', 'to continue'

There may be several steps involved in a child achieving any one over-arching outcome. Staff will need to be skilled in breaking down the outcome into achievable steps.

Outcome

Sam will consistently communicate needs and wants to the key person in focused activities and routines.

Step 1

Sam will indicate a choice by naming the preferred item from a choice of two shown by the key person during a structured activity.

Step 2

Sam will indicate a choice by naming the preferred item from a choice of two shown by the key person in all nursery activities and routines.

Step 3

Sam will spontaneously use a single word to indicate needs/wants for a preferred item when alongside the key person.

The expected impact on progress, development and/or behaviour

Staff must identify the next steps for the child; this will include the overarching outcome and any smaller steps towards this. These steps describe the achievement of the child and can be recorded as targets.

Whilst current legislation does not prescribe a national format for recording SEN support, the 2015 Code of Practice states that practitioners must keep records that include how the setting supports children with SEN and disabilities. Many local authorities and individual schools and settings have therefore devised their own to run alongside the one-page profile.

In order for the practitioner to know that the child is progressing towards the outcome, SMART targets continue to be widely used. Some now use SMARTA targets which better reflect the philosophy of a child/young person/family approach where everyone involved has played a role in agreeing the targets, rather than these being imposed.

Table 2.3 The SMART target

The general target for Iftikar	The SMART target
Iftikar will line up and go outside with the other children.	Iftikar will join the line for outside play and remain there independently for 30 seconds before an adult takes his hand to encourage him to stay and walk out with the group.
Once Iftikar achieves this SMART target one or more subsequent SMART targets may be set until Iftikar consistently and independently follows this aspect of the routine.	

S – specific

M – measurable

A – achievable

R – realistic

T – time-scaled

A – agreed

An example of how to write a SMART target is given in Table 2.3.

Provision: the interventions and support to be put into place to meet the outcomes

The early years practitioner must identify what will be provided to support the child to achieve the outcome. This may include the following:

Teaching strategies

* **Task analysis:** the process of breaking down any task into its component parts. Before teaching any new skill, the practitioner will need to identify small achievable steps towards the complete skill to be developed.

- **Chaining:** the process of teaching separate components of a task in order. The child might be taught the components from start to finish, called forward chaining, or from the endpoint in reverse order, called backward chaining. In forward chaining, the child initiates the start of the task and feels a sense of ownership. An example might be finding their shoes and beginning to put their foot in. In backward chaining, the child has the satisfaction of completing the task. An example might be where the practitioner supports the child through all stages of putting on their coat but allows the child to pull the zip up at the end.

- **Interactive/non-directive teaching:** a responsive rather than a pre-planned way of teaching that involves following the child's lead and then seeking to extend their spontaneous activity in a way that supports development of new skills. This approach is most widely used with self-directed children. For example, a practitioner might come alongside a child banging a toy on the table and begin by imitating this action. As the child pauses, the adult can then begin to bang but stops again when the child starts. In this way, the practitioner seeks to create a very simple turn-taking activity. Alternatively, the practitioner might be seeking to extend the child's experience of resources through their preference for banging. In this case, they might seek to replace the toy for a drum beater or place a drum on the table.

- **Shaping:** a teaching strategy which celebrates successful approximation of a target skill. Initially, the practitioner praises any attempt the child makes whilst demonstrating a more accurate example of the skill or response. As the child's skill level increases, the practitioner less readily praises any attempt but focuses attention on those that increasingly resemble the desired response. An example would be when a child first moves their hand to wave goodbye. Initially this may be an opening and closing of the hand held anywhere on the body. The adult celebrates that the child is 'waving bye-bye' and models a wave with an open hand at shoulder height. Gradually, as the child becomes more competent, the adult focuses on the movements that are most like a conventional wave.

- **Generalisation:** once a child has learned a skill in an isolated context, the practitioner must support the child to generalise the skill. For example, a child may learn to post a specific shape into a shape sorter but will then need to generalise the skill of posting to other toys and eventually to everyday activities such as posting a letter. Similarly, a child may learn to match using a specific matching toy and will then need opportunities to match across a range of situations so that they can gain independence to, for example, choose their own matching socks or shoes.

Nature of adult support

- **Modelling/demonstrating:** involves practitioners gaining a child's attention and engaging them to watch as they perform a task. The practitioner then encourages the child to attempt the task independently. In modelling, the practitioner leaves the resources as an example of the completed task and the child has a replica set of resources so that they can copy the model. In demonstrating, the child watches the adult and then takes the same resources from them to complete the task.

Practitioners need to ensure that a child remains focused by limiting distractions, maintaining an engaging manner through use of voice and expression and being sensitive to the child's need for repetition or a change of pace.

- **Prompting:** refers to the practitioner's role in supporting the child to complete a task. One or more of the following prompts might be appropriate:
  - Physical prompts: these may range from a full hand-over-hand prompt to a light touch to initiate a movement. Physical prompts provide a clear idea of what is expected and enable the child to experience the movements involved in the task. An example might be encouraging a child to eat, where the practitioner holds

the child's hand to the spoon handle and supports the child to scoop and lift spoon to mouth.

- ○ Gestural prompts: these do not involve physical contact but gestures to direct the child to complete the task. Gestures might include pointing, tapping to indicate the appropriate place or miming the next action. In our example, the practitioner might point to the spoon and once the child is holding, tap the bowl to indicate where to put it before miming the scooping action to prompt the movement.

- ○ Verbal prompts: these provide the child with verbal clues to complete the task. The practitioner needs to limit their language to a few carefully selected words which indicate the required action or resource to be used. Continuing the above example, the practitioner might name the 'spoon' and then the 'bowl' followed by the word 'scoop' to encourage the action.

Physical and gestural prompts should be accompanied by the verbal prompt. Gradually, physical and gestural prompts will be reduced. Reducing prompts is called fading. The practitioner should seek to fade prompts until the child can complete the task unaided.

- **Praise and rewards:** the practitioner needs to know and understand what motivates the child to ensure that they have both the incentive to engage and reward for completing task. Initially, practitioners are likely to use extrinsic rewards, which are external to the task; they involve the child receiving something they value and include being able to choose a preferred toy or activity, time with a preferred peer or adult, positive attention or verbal praise to celebrate their achievement. Intrinsic rewards lie within the child's response to the task and are realised when the child gains a sense of success, enjoyment and self-belief as they engage with and complete the task.

- **Errorless learning:** involves the practitioner creating a situation in which the child always achieves success. It contrasts with trial and error learning and is very useful for children who lack confidence or fear failure. The practitioner uses a combination of teaching strategies, prompts and rewards to present the task and support the child's success. Once the child is intrinsically rewarded, the practitioner needs to balance the reduction of their support with the need for continuing success until the child is completely independent in the task.

Other key factors

- **Child ratio:** this will specify the level of adult attention required and whether the child can be supported individually or in a small group.

- **Resources:** practitioners will need to specify the particular resources required and identify where any modifications are required.

- **The learning environment:** practitioners will identify the type of environment that best supports engagement and concentration. It may that a child needs a quiet space or calm lighting.

- **Communication:** practitioners should agree the level of language to be used, the use of a different language such as BSL (alternative communication) or the use of any signs and symbols to support understanding (augmentative communication). It is also important when implementing some targets to agree the consistent use of certain words, such as when encouraging a particular behaviour. Staff may typically use a range of phrases such as 'good/great/well done/ what a star' so that the child hears several different words without being fully aware of their meaning. If all staff agree to say 'good' followed by naming the behaviour, 'good sitting', 'good sharing', 'good looking', the child receives consistent feedback as well as labelling of the desired behaviour.

Review

A review date should be agreed and adhered to, so that progress can be monitored and an endpoint reached (monitoring and endpoint). Outcomes and targets will have been agreed within a specific timescale

SEN Support Plan				
Name of Child:		DoB:	Plan Number:	Date started:
Setting:		SEN Support Plan Co-ordinator:		
Outcomes identified with parents:				
Expected progress of the child in relation to agreed outcome(s) (Current SMART target)	**Details of the interventions/ support and how this will be implemented – provision**	**Date of Review:** **Effectiveness of the intervention and the child's response to it:**		
		Achieved/Partly Achieved /Not Achieved Comment:		
		Achieved/Partly Achieved /Not Achieved Comment:		
		Achieved/Partly Achieved /Not Achieved Comment:		

Figure 2.3 SEN support plan

culminating with the review. In order to contribute effectively to the review, the SENCo and key person will bring information relating to it, detailing the effectiveness of intervention and support in place. Throughout the period of SEN support, staff will monitor the child's response to the provision in order to summarise progress. This progress will be recorded at the review and should inform next steps as the assess, plan, do, review cycle continues.

Education, health and care (EHC) plan

The purpose of an EHC plan is to detail the special educational provision to meet the special educational needs of a child and to secure the best possible outcomes across education, health and social care.

Education, health and care plans replaced statements of special educational needs from September 2014. They differ from statements by being entirely child-centred and by detailing not only educational needs and support but also any health and social care needs which impact on the child's access to education and their learning and development and in turn the health and social care support that a child with SEND requires to reach identified educational outcomes. These plans are for children who have a disability or special educational needs that cannot be met by support that is typically available in education settings. Typically, available support must be detailed in the 'Local Offer'. Since the implementation of the Children and Families Act 2014, each local authority has been required to develop a Local Offer which is accessible to all its citizens and describes the facilities and services available to all children and young people with SEND across the public, private and voluntary sector. Each early years setting and school is a key contributor to the Local Offer as it will deliver accessible and inclusive provision for all children (see Chapter 4). The graduated approach of the SEND Code of Practice 2015 which must legally be implemented by all settings is part of the Local Offer and any child with SEND must have their needs addressed by this for a period of time before it can be agreed that support and provision beyond the Local Offer might be needed. The Children and Families Act states that an education, health and care plan is a plan specifying:

- the child's or young person's special education needs

- the outcomes sought for him or her

- the special educational provision for him or her
- any health care provision reasonably required
- any social care provision reasonably required.

Each local authority has been responsible for designing the format of their EHC plan in collaboration with children, young people and families, but legislation requires that it include the elements listed above.

Statutory assessment

The majority of young children with SEN or disabilities will have their needs met through the Local Offer in local mainstream early years settings. But:

> Where, despite the setting having taken relevant and purposeful action to identify, assess and meet the special educational needs of the child, the child has not made expected progress, the setting should consider requesting an education, health and care needs assessment.
> (DfE 2015:5.49).

Children with long-term complex needs may require an education, health and care (EHC) assessment in order for the local authority to decide if it is necessary for it to make provision for the child in accordance with an EHC plan.

Requesting an EHC assessment

For a child in an early years setting, the request for an EHC assessment can be made by:

- the child's parent or adult with parental responsibility
- a person acting on behalf of the educational setting
- other lead professionals involved with the child.

In most cases, the role of the early years practitioner will be to contribute to completing the request in collaboration with other professionals involved with the child. To support the local authority to make a decision about the child's needs, early years practitioners need to provide:

- evidence of the child's academic attainment or developmental milestones and rate of progress;

- information about the nature, extent and context of the child's SEN;

- evidence of the action already taken by the setting to meet the child's SEN;

- evidence that where progress has been made, it has only been as the result of much additional intervention and support over and above that which is usually provided;

- evidence of the child's physical, emotional and social development.

Where settings effectively implement the EYFS and SEND Code of Practice, this information will have been collected over time and can be collated to provide the required evidence for the request. Each local authority will provide guidance on how this needs to be presented. Many now have a specific EHC assessment request form for use by professionals making the request.

The local authority must then decide whether or not to proceed with an EHC needs assessment, and must inform the child's parents of their decision within a maximum of six weeks from receiving the formal request. The local authority must give their reasons if a decision is taken not to proceed with an assessment. Lack of evidence may often be a reason for not carrying out an assessment, so the role of the early years practitioner in ensuring there is sufficient and high-quality evidence is crucial.

During the assessment

When proceeding with an assessment, the local authority must collect advice from all the professionals involved with the child, as well as from the child and parent(s) to support the development of an appropriate child-centred plan. The early years setting will be required to provide 'educational advice' and each local authority will circulate a form requesting the relevant information. All practitioners should be aware that there will be legal deadlines for the return of this advice, which is within a maximum of six weeks.

The majority of educational advice forms will require the professionals to expand upon the information given at the request stage and to provide detailed short- and long-term outcomes for the child. In addition, professionals will be required to detail the provision required to deliver the outcomes and the appropriate placement for the child's ongoing education. Early years practitioners who know the child best can effectively contribute this information even where they are not the professional completing the form. For example, a nursery school head teacher will draw on the knowledge of the SENCo and class teacher and a private nursery setting proprietor may ask the SENCo and key person to provide the information required. In addition, early years practitioners may be able to support parents to tell their child's story and express their aspirations for their child.

Issuing an EHC plan

Local authorities must issue a draft EHC plan within 18 weeks and this will be shared with the parents/carers of the early years child, as well as with any professionals who have contributed advice towards its development. The role of the early years practitioner/SENCo will be to ensure that the plan accurately tells the child's story to date, reflects their strengths and needs and describes the provision and placement to meet these needs. In many cases, as the professional with the most significant involvement with parents, early years staff will play a key role in supporting them to understand the plan and to reflect on whether or not they are satisfied with it. Anyone involved with the child has a right to request amendments to the plan and, most significantly, parents and carers must consent to the draft being issued as a final plan.

At any meeting to discuss and agree amendments to a draft EHC plan, parents have the right to request a personal budget. This means that they may wish to be allocated some of the financial resources identified in the plan and have this transferred to a bank account in their name which is uniquely for the EHC provision. Where this is agreed by the local authority, they will then be able to spend the money to purchase specifically agreed elements of the provision identified in the plan. Any early years setting will need to know where parents have a personal budget and to understand which aspects of the plan they will be responsible for delivering and which lie within the personal budget. It is the responsibility of parents to access the support for their child.

A final EHC plan must be issued within two weeks of the draft being considered and amended and this must also be within twenty weeks from when the request for assessment was made. A copy of the plan will be made available to the educational setting that the child will attend.

Implementing the plan

Where children remain in their mainstream EYFS placement, the staff there must ensure that the plan is implemented as specified. Many settings will continue to use one-page profiles and target sheets to detail the delivery of the support the child requires to achieve both the long- and short-term outcomes described in their plan.

Review of plan

All education, health and care plans are subject to a formal annual review process. This review cycle is often reduced to a six-month time period for pre-school children as the rate of developmental change is great in the early years and children can make multiple transitions. They may begin with home teaching, move to a PVI sector setting and then into a maintained school nursery or reception class, all within a space of three years. Early years practitioners will be required to bring their knowledge of the progress of the child and changing needs to each review.

Conclusion

Special educational needs and disabilities remain the responsibility of all practitioners in early years settings, who have a duty to recognise where a child's development may be delayed or disordered, and take steps to ensure that s/he receives the support needed. Where a need is confirmed, the graduated approach of the 2015 SEND Code of Practice must be followed, in partnership with parents and other relevant professionals.

> Early identification of needs and the timely provision of appropriate support, together with high aspirations, can help ensure that the vast majority of children who have SEN or disabilities can achieve well and make a successful transition into adulthood.
>
> (DfE 2014b:3).

Further reading

Tutt, R. and Williams, P. (2015) *The SEND Code of Practice 0–25 years: policy, provision and practice.* London: Sage.

Department for Education (2014) *Early years: guide to the 0 to 25 SEND Code of Practice: Advice for early years providers that are funded by the local authority.* Available at: www.gov.uk/government/uploads/system/uploads/attachment_data/file/350685/Early_Years_Guide_to_SEND_Code_of_Practice_-_02Sept14.pdf

Working with parents, carers and families

Chris Collett

This chapter looks at:

- the importance of working effectively with parents
- the rhetoric and reality of working in partnership
- key principles in understanding and working with parents of children with SEND
- facilitating parents' rights, choice and control in the context of the new legislation

The importance of working with parents

Back in 1974, Mary Warnock and her committee recognised the importance of partnership with parents in supporting children with SEND by devoting a whole chapter of their report to partnership and rights (DES 1978). As is often the case, what is identified as good practice for children with SEND is also good practice for all children, and during the last thirty years, parent partnership, parental involvement and parental engagement have come to the forefront of education policy for all children. However, this broadening out has led to a construction of parent partnership that serves mainly to support practitioners, educationalists and ultimately policy-makers in raising achievement, meeting targets and academic goals and, ultimately, in realising policy objectives. This has given rise to unhelpful rhetoric around what are deemed to be 'good' and 'bad' parents, setting up a potentially adversarial relationship between 'us' (practitioners) and 'them' (parents/carers). This can be described as a deficit approach, which assumes that parents know little and need professionals to explain what their children need. The deficit approach does not value contribution from the parental perspective, other than to enable the child to be a 'better' pupil, through cooperation regarding attendance, homework, and so on.

Working with the parents of children with SEND (and indeed any parents) should avoid such a position and instead create a mutually supportive relationship that benefits the child, parents and then the practitioner/setting. This partnership approach is less didactic and more inclusive. It assumes a basis of knowledge to be shared on both sides and works towards developing an ongoing dialogue for the benefit of the child's learning.

Fixed ideas about what 'progress' and 'achievement' mean for children are also unhelpful. For many children with SEND, 'achievement' will not always manifest itself in a visible, measurable way. For children with severe and complex needs, progress may be about simply widening experiences and enabling them to enjoy an enhanced quality of life. Raised achievements should be a happy by-product of parent partnership, not its sole purpose.

All children are different; all families are different

As discussed in the Introduction, the early years environment provides unrivalled opportunities for getting inclusion right and setting a positive precedent for what is to come, for both disabled and non-disabled children. It is a chance to build strong and supportive relationships with all parents that help them to understand, and be confident about, inclusion. Now is a potentially troubling time to be a parent of a disabled child, when services – in education and beyond – are being cut, and parents may have justifiable anxieties around their child's future. Families in the twenty-first century often have complex structures and children may be looked after by foster carers, grandparents or other family members; they may have step-parents or same-sex parents. For the purposes of this chapter, the term 'parents' refers to anyone who has primary caring responsibilities for the child.

Few practitioners would dispute the fact that all children are different from each other; some – we might add – more than others! However, what we also need to remember is that parents too come in all shapes and sizes, and with different hopes and expectations for their child, based on their own age, experience, culture and beliefs. This is the same for all parents, whether or not their child has additional needs, therefore as our approach to children is an individualistic one, so should be our approach to parents, and we should avoid making assumptions about what parents might be thinking or feeling. As we recognise children's strengths and needs it is important also to understand that parents' strengths and needs will also differ, from each other, and over time.

As a co-ordinator of a pre-school specialist support service team, I spent a number of years making initial home visits to children who were newly referred. I quickly learned that parents had widely varying expectations of that visit. Some parents were eager to provide me with a detailed medical history of their child, including sensitive and personal information, from the very start. They may have been feeling highly emotional about their child's diagnosis and may have had a need to share their hopes and fears at a time when they also felt quite isolated, and were venturing into new and unknown territory. These parents needed immediate reassurance that my colleagues and I had a full understanding of their child and family.

Other parents were much more reserved, and more comfortable discussing the facts of what the service I represented would offer, and wanted more practical help with managing the input from different professionals, hospital appointments that were coming up, or accessing any resources they might be entitled to. What became apparent after the first few of these visits was that I would need (within professional boundaries) to adapt my approach to respond to those differing expectations in the most effective way.

What do we mean by 'partnership'?

Reflective activity

Which of these most closely describes the relationship with parents in your setting?

- Involvement?

- Engagement?

- Partnership?

- Participation?

- Collaboration?

List the ways in which parents can become involved in your setting. Where does the balance of power lie? Do parents have real opportunities to influence decision-making?

In any discussion of parent partnership, it is also important to understand what is meant by that word 'partnership', which can be interpreted in a number of ways. The word partnership in itself suggests a balanced relationship in which both parties have equal power and control; however, this is rarely achievable in the parent/professional context, and is perhaps an unrealistic aim. The 'power' that is held by practitioners within the setting consists of their extensive knowledge of: the curriculum, the setting, policies, procedures and practice and the theoretical context, including a broad knowledge of normative child development. Practitioners will also have some knowledge and experience of the children in their care, past and present. It is, of course, possible that parents will also have a knowledge of the early childhood context and of required procedures and policies, but it is unlikely that their knowledge will be as in-depth, and more often it will be quite limited. This automatically casts the practitioner as the 'expert' in a number of areas. However, the knowledge that the practitioner cannot replicate, is the extent to which parents will know almost, if not everything, there is to know about their own child. While the practitioner is equipped to make judgements about children who are developing broadly in line with developmental norms, when a child has SEND, the parents will hold much of the 'expert' knowledge (about their child's needs) and the balance of power shifts, though this can become less significant and relevant as the child gets older and progresses through education.

Empowerment is another term that is often bandied about in relation to parents, but it's not always clear how many practitioners truly understand *how* to empower parents. Taken literally, the word means 'giving power and control to', and it's important to consider the extent to which this can genuinely happen. In an early years setting there are likely to be limitations, but empowerment can occur on many different levels. For many parents, empowerment is simply about giving them the right information, so that they can assimilate it and take the appropriate action. For others, it may be about offering a more detailed explanation (perhaps on more than one occasion), to enable them to understand. Empowerment may mean having discussions with parents, and supporting them to come to a decision by asking questions and listening, perhaps pointing out the pros and cons of different alternatives. This must be differentiated from making the decision for them! There may also be occasions when the practitioner is required to advocate for parents, which may involve speaking on their behalf at meetings where they do not feel confident to do so, listening and taking notes in case they have questions afterwards. Wall (2011:70) reminds us that 'there are still some parents who feel intimidated or uncomfortable interacting with professionals, for a wide variety of reasons'.

In order to truly empower parents, it's also important to be aware of some potential pitfalls, summarised by MacNaughton and Hughes (2011):

- **Silencing:** this is not literally preventing parents from speaking up, but showing through our behaviour that what parents have to say is of little or no value and so deterring them from expressing views. This is particularly important for parents who may be less confident in the first instance.

- **Homogenising:** as was discussed earlier, it is vital not to think of parents as a single group, all sharing the same characteristics, but to recognise differences.

- **Essentialising:** equally it is important to not make assumptions about parents based on one particular aspect of their identity, such as ethnic background or profession.

- **Privileging:** in this context refers to early years practitioners seeing themselves (and therefore what they have to say) as being more important in the parent/practitioner relationship.

- **Knowledge and power:** making sure that we as practitioners are not 'precious' about what we share with parents, and that we do not withhold information in a deliberate attempt to remain at an advantage.

- **Cultural differences:** there may be differences between the beliefs, values and expectations held within the setting, and those held by parents, so it is important to acknowledge and respect these differences whilst seeking ways in which these can be bridged.

Parent partnership and SEND

> *Throughout identification, assessment and reviewing of SEND provision, parents have a right and duty to participate fully, but they can only really do this if they are given the appropriate information about the people, systems and processes they are engaging with, and if professionals truly listen to them.*
>
> Wall (2011:67)

Since the Warnock committee recognised the importance of parental involvement back in 1974, parents have had an influential role in shaping education of children with SEND. Cunningham and Davis

(1985, in Devarakonda 2013:146) offer three models of partnership which illustrate this increasing influence:

- **The expert model (pre-1981)** in which the professionals are the 'experts' and hold the necessary knowledge about all children with SEND. Parents are expected to passively follow the advice of the professional, due to their corresponding lack of knowledge.

- **The transparent model (1981–2015)** in which the professionals remain responsible for making decisions about the child, but parents are given enough information to participate in decision-making, and are 'trained up' to follow up on interventions at home.

- **The consumer model (2015 forward)** in which parents are presented with the available options for their child and are empowered to be the key decision-makers.

The 1981 Education Act (DES 1981) gave parents the right to have their views considered in securing an educational placement for their child, and to challenge decisions made about their child, through the SEN tribunal. In the 2001 SEN Code of Practice, parents' role in the decision-making process was further clarified and local authority parent partnership services were introduced, to support parents and to mediate any disputes. Following the 2001 code there was a long period before the education of children with SEND was reviewed, but one of the key triggers for this was the growing dissatisfaction of many parents about how their children were being served by the mainstream education system. Inclusion policy at the turn of the twenty-first century had seen the closure of a number of special schools, but parents who saw their children failed by the mainstream system, lobbied to halt the programme of closure and were largely successful. There was increased recognition that the statutory assessment process was no longer fit for purpose, and Mary Warnock had weighed in to declare inclusion policy 'disastrous' (see also Chapter 1). As an outcome of all this, Brian Lamb MP led a review of SEND provision, during which efforts were made to find out from parents what they wanted for their children. The Lamb Inquiry helped identify a number of key issues for parents that were published in a Green Paper 'Support and Aspiration' (DfE 2011).

These included:

- late identification of children's needs;

- low expectations of what children with SEND can achieve at school;

- not enough or not the right information to enable parents to make informed choices;

- limited opportunity – despite the rhetoric – for parents to make choices and decisions for their child;

- the need to negotiate different aspects of support, e.g. education/ health, separately, with a number of different professionals;

- the need for frequent repetition of background information to a number of different professionals;

- too much bureaucracy, leading to a limited understanding of how the system works.

(DfE 2011:4)

Ofsted (2010) had also noted that many parents of children with SEND experienced an 'adversarial' approach from professionals, and spoke in terms of having to 'battle' or 'fight' the system in order to secure appropriate resources for their child. As a consequence of all this, the new legislation of the 2015 Code of Practice aims to put parents and families at the centre, giving parents, in theory at least, more of a say over what services they access for their child, and how. The Local Offer sets out those services that are available, and the additional option of personal budgets gives parents choice. But at a time when cuts to services are sweeping, it remains to be seen how effectively this will be delivered.

Parent partnership in practice

The Code of Practice 2015 requires practitioners to 'listen and understand when parents express concerns about their child's development'

(DfE 2015:79). One of the key factors in working successfully with parents of a child with SEND is the ability to put yourself in their shoes. Even if you are yourself the parent of a disabled child (which is rare), each individual situation is different, and you cannot possibly know what the parent is feeling. However, you can seek to try and understand, to empathise and to respond accordingly. Practitioners' professional experience of children with SEND will fall broadly into two circumstances; a child with a SEND who comes into the setting already identified or diagnosed, or a child whose needs are identified by practitioners in the setting (see also Chapter 2). For those children in the first category, the balance of power will often (though not always) lie with the parents. They are already aware that their child has a SEND. Especially with the easy access of the Internet, there will probably have been an opportunity to research that SEND and there may well be other specialist agencies already involved who are supporting parents and sharing additional information. Not only do these parents know their child, as other parents do, they also know about the impact of his or her specific condition or disability and thus will understand their child's likely strengths, and the most effective way of supporting their needs. There may be particular areas of focus, and situations to be avoided. An effective practitioner will recognise this and both offer support to parents and also draw on them as a valuable resource, perhaps inviting them to share their specialist knowledge through a training session for staff and even for other children and parents. Some parents may be confident enough to deliver a session, whilst others may prefer to discuss the content, to enable a member of staff to deliver. Where a child has specific care needs, it may be appropriate for the parent to model strategies to staff, and even an informal Q&A session will be helpful, and will reassure parents that all staff are committed to doing the best they can for the child.

It is also important to be aware that parents of a child with diagnosed need will, one way or another, be coming to terms with having a child with a disability. This process has frequently been described as a grieving process that follows the same emotional stages as any other bereavement; denial and anger giving way to sadness and then acceptance. Every person, and therefore every parent, will move through these stages at a different rate and in their own individual way and the effects should not be underestimated. Grief can also reassert itself each time a new milestone is 'missed'; walking unaided, toilet training, the first day at primary school, all have the power to remind parents of a disabled child that he or she is taking a different and unexpected path through life. This may well be coupled with anxieties about what the future holds for their child. Practitioners therefore need to be sensitive to how parents might be feeling about their child's disability at any one time. And as with any parent, listening, instead of talking to or at them is a key component of communication.

When, on the other hand, it is the setting staff who first raise concerns about a child's development, this is likely to be the first time that parents encounter someone describing their child as different from other children, and less than 'perfect', and they will therefore be beginning that grieving process. I have often heard practitioners complain that parents are 'in denial' about a child's needs, which implies a deliberate and stubborn refusal to accept these differences. Of course, it can be frustrating to know that a child would benefit from extra support, but be thwarted in accessing this by what can seem like uncooperative parents. But in situations like this it is absolutely vital to keep lines of communication open, and tread very carefully, while allowing parents the time they need to 'catch up' with this new understanding. Parents who feel under pressure in this situation may respond by removing their child from the setting, which can only be detrimental to all those involved, especially the child. This grieving process was well described by Emily Perl Kingsley in 1987 and is widely known, but is no less powerful for its familiarity.

Welcome to Holland

I am often asked to describe the experience of raising a child with a disability – to try to help people who have not shared that unique experience to understand it, to imagine how it would feel. It's like this . . .

When you're going to have a baby, it's like planning a fabulous vacation trip – to Italy. You buy a bunch of guide books and make your wonderful plans. The Coliseum. The Michelangelo David. The gondolas in Venice. You may learn some handy phrases in Italian. It's all very exciting.

After months of eager anticipation, the day finally arrives. You pack your bags and off you go. Several hours later, the plane lands. The stewardess comes in and says, "Welcome to Holland."

"Holland?!?" you say. "What do you mean Holland?? I signed up for Italy! I'm supposed to be in Italy. All my life I've dreamed of going to Italy." But there's been a change in the flight plan. They've landed in Holland and there you must stay.

The important thing is that they haven't taken you to a horrible, disgusting, filthy place, full of pestilence, famine and disease. It's just a different place. So you must go out and buy new guide books. And you must learn a whole new language. And you will meet a whole new group of people you would never have met.

It's just a different place. It's slower-paced than Italy, less flashy than Italy. But after you've been there for a while and you catch your breath, you look around . . . and you begin to notice that Holland has windmills . . . and Holland has tulips. Holland even has Rembrandts.

But everyone you know is busy coming and going from Italy . . . and they're all bragging about what a wonderful time they had there. And for the rest of your life, you will say "Yes, that's where I was supposed to go. That's what I had planned."

And the pain of that will never, ever, ever, ever go away . . . because the loss of that dream is a very, very significant loss.

But . . . if you spend your life mourning the fact that you didn't get to Italy, you may never be free to enjoy the very special, the very lovely things . . . about Holland.

Initial contact

A good early years setting will, from the beginning, build positive relationships with *all* parents, so paving the way for future conversations, however difficult or sensitive these might be. Whether the child with SEND is coming newly into the setting, or whether staff in the setting have raised a developmental concern, there will need to be an initial discussion with parents to consider a way forward.

A reasonable time should be allowed for parents to discuss their hopes, concerns and fears, but it is equally important to tactfully make parents aware of time limits on this meeting (an hour would seem fair and substantial), whilst making it clear that this will be the first of many meetings. If the child is coming into the setting with a named condition, it may be helpful for the practitioner to undertake some research before the meeting, to give an idea of any specific terminology or characteristics the parent/carer might refer to. There is a list of possible sources of information at the end of Chapter 4.

The way in which information is recorded during these initial conversations should be governed, if possible, by parental preferences. Parents who are coming to terms emotionally with a diagnosis can find a formal approach helpful; completing paperwork or writing notes can support a more objective discussion. For other parents, making any kind of written notes can seem impersonal and even intimidating and can inhibit a full discussion. It's a good idea to have a notebook and pen to hand, but to be prepared to discard these if necessary during the meeting, and instead note down the key points immediately afterwards.

Parents may already be experiencing, or be about to experience, a range of practical difficulties for which support can be offered. There are frequently hidden costs involved in having a disabled child, for things like heating, housing, clothing and transport. Especially for children with complex needs, there is an absence of available affordable and appropriate childcare. It's possible too that a family may have more than one child with particular support needs. And parents who are themselves disabled may experience additional and very specific challenges when trying to find childcare for their children. Wall (2011) highlights other potential barriers to a productive working relationship with parents that practitioners need to be aware of. These include low self-esteem, inflexibility and/or hours of employment, social deprivation and poverty, along with more obvious cultural and language barriers.

Reflective activity

* What is meant by 'hard to reach' parents?

* Within your setting, what might be some of the barriers to working with parents?

Depending on the child's needs, parents may have a different perspective along with different expectations and priorities, in terms of what they would like for their child. For example, whilst the setting's priority might be meeting phonics targets, the parents may prefer that their child is learning to put his or her coat on independently. At times, parents and practitioners will need to be flexible and negotiate goals. Above all, parents of a child with SEND need to feel the same confidence as other parents that their child will be cared for, nurtured and afforded the same opportunities to progress as other children in the setting. Wall (2011) points out that most children will have spent the years before early years education with their parents and carers, so the transition into the setting is a big and potentially traumatic experience for both child and parents. Where a child has an additional need, parents may lack confidence in the ability of others to care for their child. At the same time, practitioners may feel additional responsibility and may feel unsure about supporting a child with those needs. There are likely to be anxieties on both sides so it is crucial that the induction process is carefully planned to alleviate those anxieties. The key to all of this is effective and ongoing communication.

Communication with parents

Providers must enable a regular two-way flow of information with parents and/or carers.

(DfE 2014b)

These days, there are a number of different ways in which practitioners communicate with parents. Face-to-face is the ideal, and there are some occasions, such as when raising a concern, that this should be non-negotiable. But when parents may be working or have additional caring commitments, and practitioners are also busy, frequent meetings may not always be possible. If communicating with parents in writing, be it in a home/nursery diary or by email, to deliver a specific message, then wording and tone are important. If the practitioner is contacting parents about a problem, pressure of time may mean it's tempting to launch into it straight away, but it is always more helpful to begin with something positive about the child. A written message, once sent, cannot be un-sent and so should be entirely professional. It is a mistake to put anything in a written message that you would not want other people to read, or that you would not be prepared to say face-to-face to that person.

The SEN Code of Practice toolkit (DfES 2001b) detailed some principles that are still relevant and useful in thinking about how we work with parents of children with SEND. In these, practitioners are encouraged to:

- create a culture of cooperation

- value parents' contributions

- follow key principles in communicating

- acknowledge and draw on parents' expertise

- focus on the child's strengths as well as needs

- recognise the personal and emotional investment of parents

- ensure that parents understand procedures

- respect differing views

- recognise the need for flexibility in timing/structure of meetings.

Parents and parents

A significant barrier to inclusion, especially where a child has a particular need that is not readily visible and can impact on his/her behaviour, can be the resistance of other parents in the setting. Young children form their beliefs and values, including their understanding of difference, in the first instance from the messages they are given by important adults around them. It is therefore crucial right from the start to make it clear to all parents that yours is an inclusive setting that welcomes all children, and encourages an acceptance of difference. Some parents might not wholly agree with this, or might agree in principle, but have a change of opinion if, in practice, this appears to disadvantage their child. Practitioners therefore need to be able to offer a sound rationale for inclusion based on the rights and opportunities of all children (see Chapter 1).

Of course, it is the duty of practitioners to keep all children safe, though this may occasionally be challenged by any child. Should such a challenge result from the actions of a child with additional needs, it is essential that this child is not stigmatised due to his/her SEND. The setting needs to have a robust behaviour management policy that all parents are familiar with, and be able to implement specific strategies to support individual children, to prevent such incidents. Chapter 8 provides further guidance. If reporting an incident with another child to parents, the name of the other child should never be disclosed, and practitioners should make sure to have all the facts of the incident and report it as objectively as records would be written in an incident log. A reminder of the behaviour policy will reassure parents that steps are being taken to prevent a recurrence.

Parents and the statutory assessment process

As we saw at the beginning of this chapter, the current legislation follows a consumer model of parent partnership, meaning that parents are seen as being key decision-makers in matters that affect their child. This will mean involvement in assessment, monitoring and the reviewing process, and is crucial:

- in the drawing-up of personalised learning plans for 'SEN support';

- in requesting, or contributing to the request for statutory assessment;

- during the statutory assessment process.

And, at such times, the 2015 SEND Code of Practice (DfES 2015:19) requires that local authorities take account of the 'wishes and feelings of the child or young person, *and the child's parents* [my emphasis]' and that both child and parents are enabled to participate *as fully as possible* in decision-making. This may include important decisions about which educational setting the child will move to, after their time in the early years setting.

Parents need to be sufficiently informed and supported to be able to do this, and it may fall to the practitioners – key worker and/or SENCo – to offer such support.

Parent carer forums

Central to the strategy of giving parents more of a voice in SEND are the parent carer forums. These are local, representative groups of parents who work alongside local authorities, education, health and other service providers to *ensure the services they plan, commission, deliver and monitor meet the needs of children and families*. These have been established in many local areas and local authorities are 'actively encouraged' to work with them (DfE 2015:22).

Early support

Available since 2004, Early Support is a national programme designed to support *the better delivery and coordination of services for disabled children, and their families*, and the professionals who may be working with them, through a range of administrative tools and information booklets (DfE 2015:82). It gives guidance to agencies on how they should work with families and is relevant to those working in health, education and social care and supports the more effective delivery of services. One of the purposes of the initiative was to reduce the repetition of information that parents can be caught up in. The Code of Practice (2015:52) requires that where possible *there should be a 'tell us once'* approach to sharing information during the assessment and planning process, so that families and young people do not have to keep repeating the same information to different agencies, or different practitioners and services within each agency. But Early Support is heavily reliant on documentation, and whilst it may be suitable for some families, parents will have varying capacities to adequately access the materials.

Conclusion

In order to effectively support a child with SEND, it is essential to have the skill and empathy to also work effectively in collaboration with the child's parents. Parents must be recognised as the experts they are, certainly in understanding their child, and often in understanding how their child can be helped. One of the key areas of knowledge essential to early years practitioners, is who can be contacted for support with different aspects of SEND. The next chapter will explore where, and from whom, help can be accessed.

Further reading

MacNaughton, G. and Hughes, P. (2011) *Parents and Professionals in Early Childhood Settings.* Maidenhead: Open University Press.

Tassoni, P. (2015) (2nd edn) *Supporting Children with Special Needs.* London: Hodder

Wall, K. (2011) (3rd edn) *Special Needs and Early Years: a practitioner's guide.* London: Sage.

Who can help?

Chris Collett

This chapter looks at:

- the nature of multi-agency working

- the role of the different sectors in service delivery, and the changing dynamics in the context of austerity measures

- the importance of working effectively with colleagues and other professionals, in the setting and beyond, to support children with SEND

- the role of multi-agency working in assessment, identification and intervention for children with SEND

- sector services/organisations who can help

This chapter will explore the statutory and voluntary sector organisations who can offer support to children with special educational needs and disabilities, their families and practitioners/settings. It will help practitioners to understand the changing roles and dynamics of different service sectors, in the climate of shrinking public funding and in the context of the Local Offer. It will also explore wider issues of inclusion and participation for children with SEND within the local community. There are a number of different terms used to describe professionals working together. The most commonly used, and the one that will be used throughout this chapter is 'multi-agency working'.

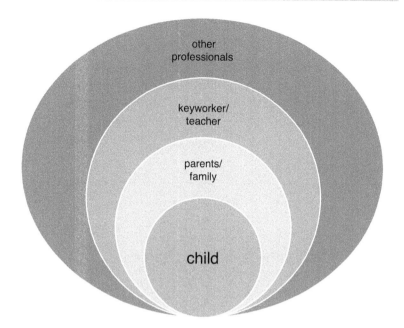

Figure 4.1 Agents for the child

So, what exactly does that mean? Taken at its most literal, the term 'agency', means simply 'action'; thus, the agents in a child's life are the 'actors', or those who act on his or her behalf (Figure 4.1).

Wall (2011) suggests that there are a number of different ways in which professionals can work together, hence the subtle differences in terminology used.

- Collaborative working: professionals working together.

- Inter-agency/interdisciplinary: professionals working in parallel, but in a more cooperative way.

- Multidisciplinary/multi-professional/multi-agency working: a number of professionals working to support the child, but not necessarily together across professional boundaries – each providing their piece of the puzzle.

• Transagency/transdisciplinary: the implementation of a keyworker system with one professional taking responsibility for coordination, and regular meetings taking place to share information, discuss progress and set joint goals.

Adapted from Wall (2011)

Reflective activity

Look at the descriptions given above. How do they differ in terms of benefits to children, families and professionals?

Whatever the terminology used, the aim of each should be about working together for the benefit of the child/family. Multi-agency working is most often required when children and/or their families have additional support needs. These may be social care needs, special educational needs and disabilities, or may be a combination of the two. Historically, there has been a strong tradition of multi-agency working to support socially disadvantaged children and in the fight against poverty; going back to the late nineteenth century, collaborations between social and health workers were commonplace (Cheminais 2009). The practice continued to play an important role in child protection and then safeguarding, and often the failure of multi-agency working is cited in serious case reviews, which has led to an increased focus in recent years. The non-accidental death of Victoria Climbié spawned a major policy upheaval for children's services which led to the Change for Children (Every Child Matters) agenda (DfES 2004), and the introduction of the Common Assessment Framework; a multi-agency tool for assessing the welfare needs of children and families. With changes to the political landscape, Every Child Matters has long since been abandoned, but some residual ideas remain and the concept of the multi-agency approach continues to be central to social policy.

Understanding the multi-agency context; the four sectors

Services (agencies) to support children and families fall under the three main categories of health, education and social care. Within each of these categories, services in the UK have always been delivered by a mix of three main sectors: the public or state sector; the private or business sector and the voluntary or 'not-for-profit' sector.

The role and prominence of each of these different sectors has changed over time, reflecting changing political ideas and public attitudes. For example, in the 1940s, when the National Health Service, Welfare State and universal primary education were introduced, it was felt by the Labour government of the time that the state played the most important role in supporting families in need. However, by the 1970s, the Conservative government of Margaret Thatcher felt that families should be more self-sufficient and less reliant on 'state handouts'. Public services were cut and the private sector began to play a greater part in delivery of services.

By the late 1990s and the next Labour government under Tony Blair, it was accepted that stretched public services would need to be 'supplemented', but instead of the emphasis on private services, which was not consistent with Labour's political ideology, the voluntary sector came to the fore, creating what is known as a 'mixed economy' of provision. When David Cameron and the coalition government came into office in 2010, new concerns about the economy and the financial unsustainability of public services, led to the emergence of a fourth sector, through the so-called 'Big Society': the community. These changes have resulted in a complex mix of services, with less money being spent on public services and a much greater focus on the private and voluntary sector.

So how do these sectors differ from one another, and what does this mean?

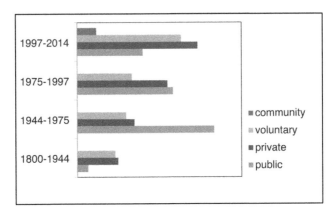

Figure 4.2 Changing dynamics of service sectors

Sector one: the statutory or public sector

The statutory sector has a responsibility to deliver the statutes (laws) enacted by Parliament and therefore consists of those services deemed essential by Government. This sector includes the National Health Service, the state education system, the national system of social care (social services) and large parts of the criminal justice system. These services are largely funded by public money (taxation) and have traditionally been free at the point of delivery. They are mainly delivered by public sector employees, although (increasingly commonly) certain functions are contracted out to private companies, for example, hospital cleaning services. These services and the people who deliver them are accountable, through inspection bodies such as Ofsted, and with an increased reliance on performance-related targets. This means that there can be a skewed emphasis on bureaucratic processes instead of genuine improved outcomes for children and families, for example the number of families using a service, might seem to be more important than the quality of support they might be receiving. Another potential disadvantage of reliance on public services in the prevailing economic climate of 'austerity', is that many services are subject to significant cuts in staffing and resources, while local councils and health trusts attempt to reduce spending. This also means that many of the services that have traditionally been delivered by the public sector are now being supplemented by private, voluntary and even community-run organisations, which bring with them their own unique pressures (see below). Examples of agencies in the public sector essential to early years settings are health visitors and social workers.

Sector two: the private sector

Services in the private (commercial) sector *sell* their goods and services, from retail goods and financial services to private education and health care. The main objective of this sector is to make a profit. Since the late 1980s, private sector services have had increasing access to Government grants through the commissioning process, in which they have the opportunity to compete with public and voluntary sector organisations, to deliver the most efficient and cost-effective service. Alongside this has come an encouragement to work in partnership with public and voluntary organisations. For example, some NHS surgical operations may be carried out by private hospitals or clinics. There are some obvious drawbacks to having services to children and families delivered by profit-seeking organisations, and rigorous inspection is needed to ensure that quality is not compromised for the sake of dividends for shareholders. There have, in recent years, been some high-profile examples of private organisations prioritising profit over quality and indeed safety. Examples of private sector services/workers that link with early years settings are private health professionals, such as speech and language therapists, private day nurseries and independent schools.

Sector three: the voluntary sector

This sector is also known as the charitable sector, voluntary and community sector (VCS), the third sector, or the not-for-profit sector. It provides services for individuals and communities that have traditionally experienced exclusion and disadvantage, and originally grew out of the charitable institutions set up during the nineteenth and early twentieth century. The title can be misleading as, these days, although a proportion of volunteer workers may be used, many organisations also employ paid staff. The 'voluntary' element is retained by having an unpaid board of trustees who oversee the activities of the organisation. The voluntary sector has undergone a great deal of change over the past ten to fifteen years, adopting a more professional approach. Services offered directly to the public may be free, but charging for them has become more commonplace (e.g. childcare). Many voluntary sector organisations have a written constitution or charitable status, and they have an additional com-mitment to campaigning on issues of social justice. A drawback of the voluntary sector can be the perception that it is 'amateur' and the residual stigma attached to making use of charitable organisations. In early years settings, there may be links with local voluntary organ-isations specific to individual children, such as the National Autistic Society, or local voluntary organisations offering broader support, such as the Trussell Trust.

Sector four: the community

In the twenty-first century in England there has been a trend for *all* political parties to develop policies that involve 'the community'. The Big Society, first announced by David Cameron (Cabinet Office 2010), seems to have foundered, but with the reduction in resources for the other three sectors, undoubtedly communities are required and expected to do more for themselves. There are clear issues here in terms of equity. Those who can afford the time and have the confidence and skills to voluntarily fill the gaps left by local authority cuts, gener-ally live in more affluent areas and are likely to come from particu-lar backgrounds. Along with this, there have been moves to increase consultation with ordinary people, which is often referred to as 'com-munity engagement' involving 'active citizens'. For example, local residents may become active in regeneration plans. However, contributing to such consultations necessitates being aware of how and when to respond, which may in turn place limitations on the range of voices being heard.

The agencies available currently, and in the future, to support children and families with SEND may sit within any of the sectors described above, so it is important to have some understanding of the tensions that might exist for others, and why this might be.

Reflective activity

Think about the outside organisations involved with your setting. Which sector do they fall into?

What are the sector-related challenges for that organisation?

Multi-agency working and SEND

Where a child continues to make less than expected progress, despite evidence based support and interventions that are matched to the child's area of need, practitioners should consider involving appropriate specialists.

(DfES 2015:88)

This section will focus on what help is available to support children and families with SEND, which may or may not overlap with the social care agenda. In addition to their general educational needs, many children with SEND, depending on the nature of their special need or disability, will require additional input/support from professionals with specific expertise. These may be specialist medical professionals, or they may be from organisations who can offer particular support to parents. A child who is diagnosed with a condition such as Down syndrome, from birth, can begin to experience this involvement straight away, and so begins the emergence of the team around the child (TAC) or team around the family (TAF). Once again, the early years provide a unique opportunity to set the precedent for effective multi-agency working and White et al. (2010:v) recognise that 'multi-agency work is effective for under-fives, although, once children attend school, there is less emphasis on a joined-up approach'.

Multi-agency working to support children with SEND was formally embraced by the 1974 Warnock Committee and in the subsequent 1981 Education Act. At that time, multi-agency working applied to those professionals working at a local level, to support an individual child/family, but as understanding of the value of multi-agency working has grown, it has also become more prevalent and more ambitious. This changing emphasis has been reflected in the subsequent legislation supporting children with SEND and this progression in the sophistication of multi-agency working is helpfully illustrated by Frost (2005, cited in Stone and Foley 2014:13), who suggests a continuum of partnership through four levels:

- uncoordinated (free standing; agencies operating in isolation from one another)
- level 1: cooperation
- level 2: collaboration
- level 3: coordination
- level 4: merger/integration.

The Warnock Report, at level one, highlighted the benefits of agencies cooperating with one another. By 2001, and the publication of the SEN Code of Practice, the need for effective collaboration of services involved with the child and with parents, was recognised. The code promoted the active collaboration and coordination of agencies to provide 'high quality, holistic support based on a shared perspective and mutual understanding and agreement' (DfES 2001a:70). And the SEN toolkit encouraged agencies to work together to create 'seamless service' for children and families (DfES 2001b).

The 2014 Children and Families Act takes this further by using much stronger, more directive language, requiring that agencies *must* work together, not just in the local 'team around the child' but also at a much higher strategic level. Whereas previous SEN legislation has confined itself chiefly to guidelines on how existing services should work together, this legislation requires a more dynamic approach in which local authorities must continually review and plan future services and provision, based on the needs of the local population (DfE 2014b). For the first time, the education, health and care plan that is drawn up to support an individual child (replacing the statement of SEN), will also play an important strategic role in helping to shape local services. And whilst Section 25 of the act makes it a legal requirement for integrated services to promote the well-being of children with SEND, more crucially, the cost of providing these services is more explicitly shared across the health, education and social care services through joint commissioning arrangements (ibid.).

Within the setting

The 2001 Code of Practice made it clear that SEN is a matter for everyone in a setting and this has not changed. However, in each early years setting, the relationship between keyworker, SENCo and manager/leader and their role in supporting children with SEND, will vary depending upon the size and nature of the setting. In a smaller voluntary-run setting, it may be that the leader/manager is also the nominated SENCo, and has an overview of all the children that allows him/her (after the appropriate discussion with the keyworker[s]) to liaise with, and make referrals to, any outside agencies. In a larger, privately run setting that could also be part of a wider organisation, the manager,

SENCo and keyworkers might all have distinct and separate roles, so will need to find a way of working together in order to meet the needs of any children with SEND in the setting. It may also be appropriate for keyworker, SENCo or manager to take on the role 'lead professional', to coordinate support. In terms of multi-agency working, we return to the two possible scenarios discussed in Chapter 3. If a child comes into the setting already diagnosed with a SEND, background information will need to be gathered, including which other professionals/ agencies might already be involved. Whilst this information may be gathered by the keyworker, SENCo or setting leader/manager, it is then essential that this information is shared with any other relevant staff within the setting. If a child already in the setting is identified as having an additional need significant enough to require specialist help, this will necessitate referral to a specialist agency by the lead professional. More specific guidance on the assessment and early identification process can be found in Chapter 2.

The role of the special educational needs coordinator (SENCo)

In a maintained nursery school or class (one that is funded by the local authority), the SENCo must be a qualified teacher who has either the prescribed qualification for SEND coordination or relevant experience. The EYFS framework (DfE 2014b) and 2015 SEND Code of Practice also require other early years providers (in non-local authority settings) to identify a SENCo. Childminders are encouraged to identify a person to act as SENCo (which within the setting is likely to be the childminder herself!), although childminders who are registered with an agency or who are part of a network may nominate someone to share the SENCo role between them.

The role of the setting-based SENCo is to:

- ensure that all practitioners in the setting understand their responsibilities with regard to children with SEND, along with the setting's approach to identifying and meeting SEND;

- advise and support colleagues;

- ensure that parents are closely involved throughout and that their views and insights inform any action taken by the setting;

- liaise with professionals or agencies external to the setting. (DfE 2015)

Non-maintained settings will also have support from an Area SENCo who will advise and offer practical support to setting-based SENCo in implementing the graduated approach of the SEND Code of Practice; ensuring that arrangements are in place to support children with SEND; planning for children with SEND to transfer between early years provision and schools, and helping to strengthen links between the settings, parents, schools, social care and health services (DfE 2015:88–90). So what does this mean in practice?

Case study 4.1: Dylan

Dylan is born at full term in the hospital maternity ward. The midwife who delivers him recognises certain physical characteristics and at 3 hours old the paediatrician confirms that Dylan has Down syndrome and also a heart murmur. When the time is right the midwife contacts the Down Syndrome Association and asks one of their volunteers (the parent of a child with Down) to come and offer support to the parents. After a week in hospital Dylan goes home, and the health visitor comes to see them. It has already been noted that Dylan's muscle tone is floppy, so a referral is made to the community physiotherapist. His sucking reflex is weak and he seems to dribble excessively so referral is also made to the speech and language therapist. In order to make the most of any early learning opportunities, referral is also made to the local Portage home teaching service. Although he is very smiley and sociable, making lots of eye contact with those around him, after a few weeks it becomes clear that Dylan does not startle to loud sounds, or turn towards his mum when she talks to him, so a referral is made to an audiologist, to test his hearing, and then to a teacher of the deaf.

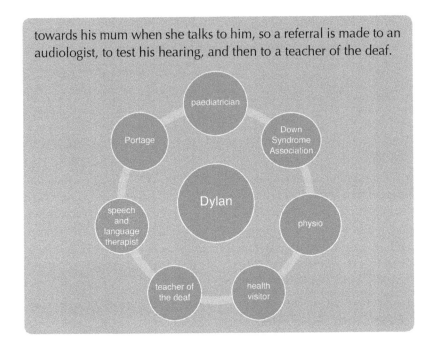

For a child like Dylan, who comes into the setting already known to outside agencies, the responsibility of the practitioner is to establish who these people might be, and build effective working relationships with them. There are key questions that can be asked at that time.

- How long have you been involved?
- What contact have you had with the child/family?
- What do you do to support the child?
- Who did you receive a referral from?
- What can we do to help?
- What have you found that the child likes/dislikes?
- Have you worked with the child at home?
- What contact do you have with [the child's] parents?

Case study 4.2: Salwa

Salwa is 4 years old and started in nursery in September. Her key-worker has noticed that she always plays alone, rarely gives eye contact or responds to instructions and never speaks. She asks the SENCo to help with some focused observations and they learn that Salwa rarely sits at any activities, preferring to wander around the room. When the keyworker speaks to Salwa's mum – who speaks good English - she discloses that she is having difficulties getting Salwa to eat and sleep at home, and that when Salwa gets upset she sometimes hits herself. There are further concerns because Salwa will be leaving the nursery in a few weeks to start school. With parents' permission, the SENCo contacts the Area SENCo, then makes a referral to the local child development centre for a multidisciplinary assessment (see below). Following the assessment, a diagnosis of autism spectrum disorder (ASD) is made, along with referrals to a number of agencies.

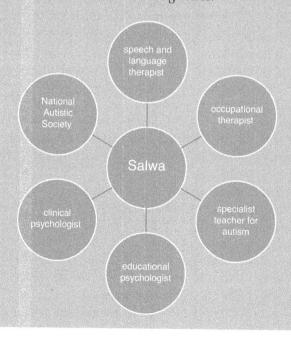

Where a child has a less complex disability that does not require a multidisciplinary assessment, it may be that the setting SENCo needs to make a referral to a specific agency or professional and create that working relationship. Sometimes it may simply be that relevant information needs to be passed on to parents. Other parents may need you to make contact on their behalf with the agency/professional (see also Chapter 3). A list of commonly used agencies is at the end of this chapter. The SEND Code of Practice (DfE 2015:80) requires that 'where assessment indicates that support from specialist services is required, it is important that children receive it as quickly as possible'. Early intervention is key, and in the current climate of reduced public services this is especially important, given that children often only remain in an early years setting for a relatively short time.

Multidisciplinary assessments

For pre-school children with multiple needs, complex needs and who may be on the autism spectrum, it is important that a thorough assessment is conducted by professionals who have specialist skills and knowledge in particular areas. Most local authorities will have specialist centres where a multidisciplinary assessment can be carried out. These centres may be referred to as child development centres (CDCs), specialist assessment centres, and so on, and may be attached to a local hospital, health centre or Sure Start centre. The child (and parents) will be invited to an assessment session, usually for a minimum of around two hours, which takes place in a room set up to replicate a nursery room. The child will be in a small group of around five or six other children, possibly with similar needs, and will be observed as s/he interacts (or doesn't) with the play equipment, other children and staff. The staff team, also in the room, will consist of a specialist teacher, specialist nursery nurse, speech and language therapist (SLT), physiotherapist, occupational therapist and, depending on the nature of the group, a clinical psychologist. As part of the assessment, the child will also have a separate appointment with a paediatrician, who will look at overall development. Following the session (or more than one), the professionals who have observed the child will meet, discuss and collate their findings into a report that includes recommendations. The child's parents will then be invited to a meeting with key professionals, to discuss the report and to plan next steps for the child. These may include returning to the CDC on a more regular basis for a therapeutic group, starting to attend a nursery or pre-school group, or being referred to community outreach services, such as speech and language therapy or physiotherapy.

If the child is already attending an early years setting, it is vital that the SENCo and/or the keyworker have the opportunity to contribute to this discussion, as they will have valuable knowledge about the child's disposition day-to-day within the setting. The contribution may be a written report submitted to the CDC as part of the assessment process, or it may be that one of the professionals from the CDC comes out to the setting to observe the child and talk to staff. This information sharing is essential as the observations made in the CDC assessment group are only a snapshot of the child in new and unusual surroundings. Similarly, it is vital that the outcomes from the assessment are shared with the setting, especially as there may be implications for the child's daily care. It should not be assumed or expected that parents will pass on information from the setting to the assessment team or vice versa. In some circumstances, it may even be helpful to parents to have a trusted practitioner from the setting to accompany them to the feedback meeting, as the nature of the discussion – particularly if there is a diagnosis – might evoke an emotional response that makes it difficult for parents to absorb the detail of all that is being explained.

Parental consent

Where a child is identified as having significant SEND, but there is no need for a CDC multidisciplinary assessment, it will be the keyworker and/or SENCo who refer the child to outside agencies. The 2015 SEND Code of Practice (p. 88) makes it clear that in early years settings, any 'decision to involve specialists should be taken with the child's parents'. And the EYFS (DfE 2014b:14) requires that providers 'have the consent of parents and/or carers to share information directly with other relevant professionals'. In any event, it is of course best practice to make any decisions in partnership with the child's parents, but it is essential to at least have parental permission.

The key to effective intervention is to begin as quickly as possible. But the current climate of sweeping cuts to services is putting pressure on already limited resources, and often means that services have lengthy waiting lists. Additionally, at the time when referral becomes necessary, parents may be at different stages of coming to terms with their child's 'difference' (see Chapter 3), and may not be ready to involve others. Practitioners at this time will need to exercise patience, and if necessary delay the referral. Once referrals are made, parents may also need to be supported to be realistic in their expectations, but also assertive when needed.

Factors for successful multi-agency working

Communication and relationships

These have been deliberately grouped together as they are so closely interlinked. The foundation for working productively with other professionals, as with parents and colleagues, is having a sound working relationship. Relationships in turn are built on having honest, open and available lines of communication. Practitioners also need to be able to communicate at different levels, and have the confidence to represent the child and parents when needed. Parents should not be required to take on the responsibility for passing on information from one agency to another, though this is often the reality. Practitioners may sometimes also be required to 'translate' any jargon or specific terminology that is used by other professionals for parents and/or colleagues, so it is important to seek clarifications from those professionals.

Understanding roles and responsibilities

This also means recognising the external pressures to which all professionals are subject, and any limitations of their role. Inside the setting, a SENCo might be undertaking the role alongside many other duties, in addition to having responsibility for groups of children throughout the day. Beyond the setting, local authority and health authorities are in disarray thanks to the 'austerity measures' introduced to cut public expenditure. Caseloads are unmanageably high, and in services where there are recruitment difficulties, such as social care, posts can be filled by temporary agency workers, meaning that relationships have to be built and rebuilt a number of times. All this can lead to frustrating delays and make it seem as if others are uninterested and disengaged, when this is rarely the case.

Commitment

The practitioner's responsibility is in the first instance to the children, then parents and finally to external professionals, and in a busy setting it can be difficult to make time for the necessary professional meetings. But there should be a commitment to meeting the needs of all the children in the setting, therefore there must be an opportunity to attend these meetings and so a commitment also needs to come from managers who can facilitate this.

Negotiation and mediation

This may be around a variety of issues, such as: negotiating with colleagues to have time to meet (see above); negotiating with the setting-based SENCo, who will take responsibility for aspects of multi-agency working; or negotiating with an external professional, who may have other priorities.

Organisation and record-keeping

At a basic level, this means recording the dates of any forthcoming meetings with or visits by other professionals, to allow for planning and preparation. And where important information is being shared amongst a number of people, often with a time lag, it is essential that records are kept of conversations and meetings, and that any actions arising from these are noted and acted on as swiftly as possible. Some of these records may also be an important part of the evidence gathering, should there be a later request for statutory assessment (see also Chapter 2).

Time and space

For all of the above to work well, more than anything else there is a need for adequate time. Time to communicate, time to build relationships, time to share information, time to keep records, time to research and understand others' roles. Often, time seems to be the resource that is in shortest supply and for practitioners in settings, it is crucial that they have the support of managers in allowing sufficient time to fulfil SEND responsibilities.

At the very beginning of this book, attention was drawn to the increased expectations on the shoulders of early years practitioners. The early years workforce, particularly in the non-maintained sector, is itself relatively transient. Neither of these factors presents optimal conditions for building expertise and confidence, or sustaining the kinds of relationships that are helpful to families where there is a child with SEND. Often, effective multi-agency working is about individual professionals doing the best they can for a child. If all works well (which rarely happens all the time), practitioners as well as the child and family will feel supported. However, any of the factors above can become barriers to effective working if they are not established and maintained.

Multi-agency working 'is about making sure that people are regularly talking about their work, understanding each others' roles and sharing with other agencies and service users. It is about working together towards commonly agreed aims and objectives' (DfE 2012).

> ## Reflective activity
>
> * If these are the factors that support effective multi-agency working, what skills and qualities do practitioners need?
> * How successful is multi-agency practice in your own setting?

Health and progress reviews

The 2014 EYFS and the 2015 SEND Code of Practice have both proposed an integrated 2-year review for all children that will combine the health and educational progress checks. The purpose of this is to:

* identify the child's progress, strengths and needs at this age in order to promote positive outcomes in health and well-being, learning and development;

* enable appropriate intervention and support for children and their families, where progress is less than expected; and

* generate information which can be used to plan services and contribute to the reduction of inequalities in children's outcomes. (DfE 2015:84–5)

This is a good example of how agencies are now expected to work together in an integrated way and will mean liaising with local health visitors for all children. Where a need is identified by either practitioners or the health visitor, information will need to be shared and any further referrals made.

Multi-agency working for SEN support and EHC plans

If a child has other agencies involved during the graduated 'SEN support' phase, it is important that their contribution to any individualised plans, such as the one-page profile, is sought. Practitioners may need to work flexibly and use their negotiation skills to achieve this. For example, if a face-to-face meeting cannot be arranged to agree these, then it may be necessary to contact the professional and request that any outcomes and interventions can be forwarded for inclusion on the plan.

If the child then goes on to have an education, health and care plan then the local authority will be responsible for convening those agencies who are likely to be involved to finalise the plan with the relevant contributions (see also Chapter 2).

The Local Offer

The 2015 Code of Practice requires that local authorities publish in one place, details of the services available in the locality for children and young people with disabilities and special educational needs. Making parents aware of what is out there is intended to give them more choice and control over what support is right for them and their child. Linked to the outcomes identified in the education, health and care plans of individual children, each Local Offer should be developed by local authorities and their service providers along with children, their parents and young people. In turn, the organisations providing services are also required to demonstrate how they meet their local authority's Local Offer. The code emphasises that the Local Offer *should not simply be a directory of existing services* (DfE 2015:60). Information is provided in the Local Offer regarding:

- special educational provision;
- childcare, including suitable provision for disabled children and those with SEN;
- arrangements for identifying and assessing SEN, including EHC assessments;
- health and social care provision;
- leisure activities;
- short-break facilities;

- travel arrangements to and from schools, colleges and early years education settings;

- sources of information, advice and support;

- arrangements for dispute, resolution, mediation and complaints.

This comprehensive resource is also designed to support parents who opt for a personal budget and wish to choose which services they access to support their child.

Sure Start Children's Centres

Children's centres have been integral to early years policy since the late 1990s, though their role and function has changed during the intervening years. Initially set up in areas of high deprivation they became more widespread as part of the New Labour strategy to address poverty and inequality. But sustainability issues have meant that in many places, children's centres have reverted to their original purpose, targeting areas of high deprivation only. There are, in consequence, fewer of them. The purpose of children's centres is to improve outcomes for young children and their families, and reduce inequalities. The focus is on disadvantaged families and will often include support for children with SEND. Sometimes incorporating early years provision, such as a day nursery, these are also centres where health, education and social care professionals work together, either based in the centre or through outreach, to support the most vulnerable children and families (Foundation Years 2016).

Conclusion

In a landscape of shrinking public services there remain key organisations who can support children with SEND and their families. It's important therefore that practitioners in early years settings are conversant with key agencies and/or know how to access the relevant information. Understanding the role and dynamics of the different sectors in which specific agencies/services are located will help to inform and secure effective working relationships with professionals from those agencies.

Agencies that can help

No one can be expected to store an exhaustive list of organisations in their head, but it will be important to have available key basic information, particularly regarding local services, and to know who they are, or where to go to find out. Review information regularly and make sure what you hold is up to date. There is nothing worse for a parent who has plucked up the courage to make that important phone call, than to then find that the number is no longer valid. Websites are often a good starting point; some have been given at the end of this chapter, and the Local Offer, published by your local authority (above) will also help.

Statutory sector agencies

Paediatrician: a doctor who specialises in treating children and infants.

Health Visitor: visits families at home offering a primary care service; advice on issues such as feeding, growth and development, toileting programmes, immunisation and child protection.

Specialist teachers: provide educational advice to parents and staff. Local authorities will have an advisory teaching service, or inclusion team made up of teachers and learning support assistants (LSAs) specialising in SEND (pre-school), communication difficulties, hearing and visual impairment.

Educational psychologist (EP): works with parents and practitioners to assess the psychological and educational needs of children with learning difficulties, and has a key role in the development of the EHC.

Social worker: provides advice, practical help and support for a child and family. Can assist in applying for benefits, home adaptations and arranging short break (respite) care.

Child and adolescent mental health service (CAMHS): supports the mental health needs of children and young people. Traditionally a service that has worked with school-age children only, in certain circumstances pre-school children may also be supported.

Speech and language therapist (SLT): works with the child to promote all areas of language development and communication. Some SLTs are also able to give specific advice on feeding.

Physiotherapist: works with the child, parents and staff providing advice and exercises for the physical development of a child. Will provide aids to mobility where appropriate.

Occupational therapist (OT): works with children and young people to develop 'life skills', particularly those requiring fine motor skills. Will provide physical aids where appropriate.

Voluntary sector agencies

Parent Link Action Project worker: offers short-term individual support within a setting to a child with SEN. Parent link workers are linked to the Pre-school Learning Alliance and support children in non-profit-making organisations and private nurseries.

Contact a Family: a good starting point, should you have a child in your setting with a diagnosed disability that you are unfamiliar with. The organisation runs an online directory providing key information about hundreds of specific disabilities and syndromes, and also gives useful details of organisations that practitioners or families can access for further information and support: www.cafamily.org.uk/

Mencap: a voluntary organisation supporting children and adults with learning disabilities and their families: www.mencap.org.uk

Scope: a voluntary organisation supporting children and adults with cerebral palsy, and their families: www.scope.org.uk/

National Autistic Society: a voluntary organisation supporting children and adults with learning disabilities and their families. There are also regional groups, such as Autism West Midlands. www.nas.org

ICan: a voluntary organisation supporting children and adults with learning disabilities and their families: http://www.ican.org.uk

Portage: provides a home visiting educational service and some other family support services in some regions of the country.

Useful websites

- National Children's Bureau: www.ncb.org.uk
- Council for Disabled Children: councilfordisabledchildren.org.uk
- National Association for Special Needs: nasen.org.uk
- Down Syndrome International: www.dseinternational.org
- Kids: www.kids.org.uk

    www.autismeducationtrust.org.uk

    www.thecommunicationtrust.org.uk/early-years/

    www.talkingpoint.org.uk/

    www.makaton.org

    www.pecs-unitedkingdom.com

Further reading

Gaspar, M. (2010) *Multi-agency Working in the Early Years: challenges and opportunities.* London: Sage.

Hodkinson, A. (2016) (2nd edn) *Key Issues in Special Educational Needs and Inclusion.* London: Sage.

Wall, K. (2011) (3rd edn) *Special Needs and Early Years: a practitioner's guide.* London: Sage.

Creating an inclusive early years setting

The key role of picture books and other resources

Karen Argent

This chapter will:

- highlight the central role of practitioners in creating a culture of accepting, valuing and celebrating difference within the setting

- explore picture books as powerful tools in raising awareness and promoting positive ideas of disability

- provide examples of specific picture books that represent particular characteristics of disability as a normal part of the social landscape

- discuss the use of wider resources to develop an inclusive learning environment

This chapter focuses on the importance of providing a wealth of positive images of SEND through the everyday selection of picture books, dolls, small world play and the wider environment. These of course need to be in the mix with resources at all times, not just because there happens to be a child with a particular condition attending the setting at a particular time. This can be challenging because there are so many variations of SEND, many of which have recognisable characteristics; for example, the distinctive facial features of many people with Down syndrome, or the use of support devices like wheelchairs and walking frames, hearing aids or guide dogs (which may be why they are sometimes represented in picture books). The less visible disabilities like dyspraxia and ASD are more challenging to depict with accuracy, although it is precisely these high incidence disabilities that are most likely to be within the experience of children attending mainstream early years settings. We now know that early experiences contribute to shaping a positive self-image and so this is why resources in early years settings can be so significant.

Indeed, Apple (2004:5) points out that all educational settings 'act as agents of cultural and ideological hegemony' and, given their role, early years practitioners play a potentially influential part in determining the ways in which these hegemonic, or dominant 'common sense' ideas and views of the world are first transmitted to children. He suggests that this early phase of education is crucial to the way that children learn how to define meaning through understanding about what is given value in society by way of both the overt and the hidden curriculum. So, all early years practitioners play a significant role in shaping the attitudes of the children they work with and, in doing so, help them to understand and make sense of a range of complex or abstract concepts and issues. One of the issues that they need to help children comprehend is the notion of exclusion – how some groups, because of their particular characteristics, are marginalised by society and its institutions. However, early years practitioners also need to go beyond this process of identification and description and begin to encourage children to engage with the reasons why this happens.

It can be all too easy for individuals in early years settings to believe that they are providing adequate 'inclusive' resources without them having an understanding of why these are so important. This is not just about complying with equality policy and relevant statutory curriculum guidance, just in case Ofsted might be looking (although this regulation is of course very important), but because it is the right of all children to be able to play freely with all the available resources, and also to ensure that they see themselves reflected in the learning environment. In any setting, such resources are regarded by parents and carers as reliable sources of information as they are provided by practitioners as part of the curriculum. It is therefore very important to realise that the initial selection and use of resources by practitioners, conveys powerful messages about what is valued and 'normal' within that setting. If the range of representations that challenge accepted social norms are *not* available, then it is likely that children will not develop what the art critic John Berger (1972) calls different 'ways of seeing'. What children don't see is therefore just as powerful as what they do see and so has significant implications for every child's perception of disability. If all they encounter in their early years learning environment are images of the non-disabled as 'normal' then the task of encouraging them to see disability as just another version of normality gets harder.

This isn't just about the children with SEND in a setting, as their parents and carers are also to be considered when providing a welcoming place that recognises and values difference with regard to children's individual needs. This is also about establishing a caring and considerate environment that gives strong messages of inclusivity to all the parents, carers, children, staff and any visitors, who perhaps have very little personal experience of SEND themselves. Providing all this to a high standard and avoiding tokenism, in other words just a superficial response to finding good-quality resources, requires that early years practitioners know where to find such resources because they are not always easily available. Part of this professional responsibility means being able to recognise gaps in provision, regularly auditing resources, and ensuring up-to-date knowledge for all staff via research and training.

Access to the learning environment

Effective inclusive practice means that all children can access all the resources equally. Ensuring that this is taken into consideration when selecting equipment and appropriate space for children with a wide and diverse range of SEND, should underpin inclusive provision and be a consideration when planning any activities. This, plus appropriate differentiation of and support for activities, should be the responsibility of the SENCo, along with all staff who are committed to providing an inclusive and enabling learning environment in line with the Disability Equality Duty (2006), which places a clear responsibility on all educational settings to have an anticipatory role in promoting inclusive, non-discriminatory practice in terms of curriculum and resources. The Statutory Framework for the Early Years Foundation Stage (DfE 2014a), which is currently used as curriculum guidance by all practitioners in early years settings, can be interpreted as attaching importance to the issue through its stated commitment to diversity:

> Providers have a responsibility to ensure positive attitudes to diversity and difference - not only so that every child is included and not disadvantaged, but also so that they learn from the earliest age to value diversity in others and grow up making a positive contribution to society.

The EYFS also identifies three 'characteristics of effective learning' in order to help practitioners recognise the importance of playing and exploring; active learning and creating and thinking critically. Anything that prevents any of these is a potential barrier to inclusion. Individual needs will vary and change over time and where there are children with SEND, any necessary modifications to the environment and resources will be part of their individual education plan and reviewed on a regular basis by staff, parents and the child. However, there are some general rules of good practice that can be applied to both the inside and outside learning environment in any setting that aims to include all children, parents, visitors and staff:

- Does the layout allow sufficient space for wheelchairs and other mobility aids?
- Can all available resources be easily reached and used?
- Can all available resources be easily seen and heard?
- Can children participate fully in making choices?
- Are you consulting with parents about what happens at home?

It is useful if all practitioners can get into the habit of asking these questions, and then taking appropriate action if there are any concerns. Sometimes, even with very careful planning it might not be obvious what the barriers to inclusion might be until a child is actually trying to access the resources.

Case study 5.1: James

Four-year-old James is on the autistic spectrum and responds best when he is in a designated quiet, carpeted part of the classroom. He never goes willingly to play with creative resources which are located in the messy play area, although his mum tells his teacher that he very much enjoys painting at home.

After this conversation and discussing with staff and children, an easel with paint pots is set up in the quiet area with plastic sheeting to protect the carpet.

After some time and with the support of the teacher, James chooses this activity on a regular basis and produces some impressive paintings.

Here we can see how the desire to keep an orderly classroom with designated areas can sometimes get in the way of chidren's learning. Does it really matter if painting takes place in a different place? Perhaps we underestimate how all children can take responsibility for being careful with paint splashes, and so on, and that, as this is washable, it doesn't really matter anyway! This example is based on a real experience, where I asked the children for the solution, using a story about a boy called Henry who had similar characteristics to James. You too might be surprised at the creative solutions proposed by even very young children when presented with a problem to solve.

Case study 5.2: Meena

Three-year-old Meena has cerebral palsy which for her means that the left side of her body is quite difficult to coordinate. She enjoys tabletop play activities but becomes very frustrated when the pieces of a jigsaw keep sliding about.

> The teacher provides some support with her play by steadying the puzzle pieces and sometimes handing them to her but soon realises that she wants to do this independently.
>
> After observing Meena on several occasions she places the pieces on a small tray fixed securely to the table with a Dycem® mat, within easy reach of her preferred right side.
>
> Staff realise that this is a very helpful modification for many other children who have fine motor difficulties and use it for other tabletop activities such as threading and small world play.

This example demonstrates how very small modifications to how the resources are organised can benefit all the children in a class. This is again based on a real experience where I asked a child's mother if she had any ideas and she told me that she had been advised to fix items in this way by the Portage service that had been supporting her child at home since she was a baby. Inclusive practice is good early years practice, so regular observations by staff and the consequent review and modification of provision in close consultation with parents and children can only improve the learning environment for everyone.

Picture books

Despite their importance as educational and cultural artefacts, some children do not see many picture books until they experience them outside the home in various early years settings. When they do encounter them, they are usually selected by adults to provide an accessible first encounter with the experience of literature. The extent to which these choices are shaped by the practitioner's own personal and professional experiences is important to understand, as is the fact that their initial and ongoing training will have helped to determine their view of the role that picture books should play in the child's educational experience. These factors have a significant influence both on the way that picture books are selected and the value they are given beyond their instrumental purpose in providing a stepping stone to books that rely on written text. Central to these choices are questions about the personal and professional values practitioners operate with and whether, as they progress in their careers, they are encouraged to see picture books as tools that can be used for conveying complex ideas to young children about difference, inequality and social justice and as resources that can be used to challenge stereotypes about gender, ethnicity, social class and disability.

These early books are very significant because they are often read and re-read with the support of these adults, providing the child with a gateway through which they can make links to their personal experiences and giving them new ways of looking at the world. They require the child to pay close attention to what is conveyed by the pictures and how these are 'explained' by the adult, but also with what lies behind the picture in terms of the subtext – and it is the adult who needs to help develop these complex perceptual and semantic interpretive skills. Sharing any picture book with a young child provides a challenging cognitive experience, no matter how simple the book may appear to be. Evans (2009:7) claims that many will have layers of meaning that may include pictorial references to other stories, twists and turns, and use of irony and humour, and points out that the 'complexity of picture books should not be underestimated'. Whitehead (2010:129) neatly captures their unique powerful quality when she says that 'the very lack of written text means that a picture book is rich in narrative spaces that must be filled by the reader.'

Picture books are recommended as a vehicle for providing what is described as an 'enabling environment' which includes 'positive images that challenge children's thinking and help them to embrace differences in gender, ethnicity, language, religion, culture, special educational needs and disabilities' (DfE 2015). So will any representation of disability help to achieve this? Not necessarily, and it is therefore necessary to think about how early years practitioners can judge whether a picture book is conveying accuracy of representation, diversity of images and variety of perspectives as well as being a good story. To help with this evaluation, Saunders (2000), from an 'insider' perspective as a mother with a disability, has produced a very useful framework for analysis that evaluates books. In order to achieve a better critical analysis, she suggests that practitioners apply what is known as the 'DICSEY' code when selecting books, to raise disability awareness in children and to explore the theme of difference. This acronym proposes that adults need to be aware of how almost any picture book conveys both overt and subliminal messages about disability, appropriate images, control, society, enabling environments and the important role of young carers. In this way, she believes that it is possible to broaden the range of books that can be used to address this issue given the relatively small numbers of books of high literary quality that deal specifically with disability. Her approach reinforces the view that 'images come from pictures and stories which only tell us part of the truth' (Saunders 2000:32), and she provides a wide number of examples of ways in which the DICSEY code can be applied by practitioners in order that they can explore notions of difference and inequality with young children.

Some examples of picture books

Richard Rieser is a well-known disability rights campaigner and educator who had polio when he was a young child, which left him with a lifelong disability. I listened to him speak at a conference many years ago and always remember him telling the story of how he had never seen a child that looked like him in a book, other than the crippled boy who gets left behind when the Pied Piper takes all the children into the Magic Mountain, in the famous story based on the poem by Robert Browning. Rieser explained that this had compounded a feeling of difference and exclusion, which we now understand can have a profoundly negative lifelong effect. It also means that the invisibility of such children in mainstream literature can give a message that they are not important and valued to other children. Times have changed and there are now certainly more images of people with physical disabilities in the media, particularly in connection with the recent Paralympics. But what about representations of ordinary people doing their shopping, going to school and having fun? What about stories where the main protagonist just happens to wear a hearing aid or be a wheel-chair user or need to go for regular visits to the physiotherapist without it being the main theme of the book? And are there sufficient represen-tations of children from a range of BME communities in this mix?

Thankfully, there are now many very good picture books being pub-lished that do all this very well, but they are not finding their way into early years settings as quickly as they should. This may be because some of the good ones are published in the USA and other countries and so they are not stocked by mainstream distributors. As a conse-quence, many practitioners may be unaware of their existence and you could play your part in bringing them to the attention of colleagues.

I have a huge collection of picture books with disability-related content that I have accumulated over many years of teaching and would like to present some of my favourites here. I will select three to review in a little more detail but I would urge you to find them and enjoy them for yourself before using them with children, because your intimate knowledge of the story will help you to use it to full effect and your enthusiasm for any one of them will be infectious. It might be that you don't like all of them in terms of the illustrative style or even the story, but remember to apply a critical eye using the DICSEY code to help you to make decisions about which ones to use. Also, keep in mind that you might be the only early years practitioner who is aware of these books in a setting and that if the children do not experience them with you, they may never ever come across them. This is quite a responsibility!

Happy Butterfly by Pippa Goodheart, illustrated by Lauren Tobia

This is a story about an exciting event in the life of a little girl who wants to join in with a Caribbean Carnival parade, and her grand-mother makes her wings to turn her into a butterfly on a float. This is not a story about wheelchairs but about a child who just happens to

Figure 5.1 Example of a picture book that includes a character with a physical disability. Goodhart, P. (author) and Tobia, L. (illustrator). (2010)

be a wheelchair user. It demonstrates that a wheelchair user can fully participate in and enjoy an ordinary community event.

The cover of a picture book will often provide a clue as to what is inside and I like the way that all of these examples give a very positive message about being active and independent, with the help of mobility aids. They also convey the way in which any child's imagination can take them anywhere. In terms of achieving a degree of social realism, it is also relevant to consider the importance of portraying up-to-date support equipment. For instance, wheelchairs are now often custom-ised in bright colours and bear little resemblance to the traditional image of institutionalised versions. An interesting journal article by Matthew and Clow (2007) discusses how there are emerging new aids and devices that illustrators may need to research in order to portray realistic social environments.

Figure 5.2 Picture books that include a character with ASD.
a: Welton, J. (author), Telford, J. (illustrator) (2015); **b:** Walsh, M. (2016)

Figure 5.2 (Continued)

Example one: *Tomas Loves* by Jude Welton

I really like the action implicit in this book title because it suggests that Tomas is going to play a central role in the following story, which it states is about 'fun, friendship and autism'. The front cover illustration that extends across the back and is repeated as the first double-page spread is also positive because it shows the little boy smiling and totally absorbed in playing with his toy train with his dog lying beside him. The following pages show Tomas and his dog, Flynn, spending time enjoying doing things like watching cars, listening to stories with the structure of repetitive content, and playing with tiny toys. This boy clearly enjoys the same range of activities and experiences as any other child. But at the same time, the book provides us with important information about his need for a calm environment, routine and planning.

Example two: *Isaac and His Amazing Asperger Superpowers* by Melanie Walsh

This is certainly a book that is specifically trying to educate its readers about this common condition and it does this very effectively. The brightly coloured naive illustrations are very pleasing throughout. I also liked the way that the wide spectrum of autism is well conveyed on the endpapers as a rainbow of colours that bleeds across from left to right. The book is written from the point of view of a young boy called Isaac who thinks of himself as a superhero with superpowers associated with his Asperger syndrome. As we read on, he gives the reader important information about some common characteristics like having a good memory for detail, repetitive behaviours, super sensitivity to noise, problems with remembering social conventions like saying 'hello', and the benefits of having an object to fidget with to improve concentration in class. These characteristics are depicted very well and with some humour, which would encourage some interesting discussion with children. In this book, the fact that the word 'Asperger' is included in the title immediately frames it as a book all about Asperger syndrome. This is further emphasised by an endorsement from The Autistic Society on the front and back covers, which could potentially limit the target audience. Is it only aimed at children and adults who want to know more about this particular condition? Perhaps I am wrong, but I would be interested to know whether the author wanted this informational emphasis or whether she would have preferred it to be just a book about a boy called Isaac with amazing superpowers, who just happened to have Asperger syndrome.

I can strongly recommend this book because it gives plenty of good examples of how children like Isaac can be very easily included into a mainstream nursery or school with a bit of care, empathy and imagination.

I suppose that the very best inclusive picture books that include a positive portrayal of characters with disabilities are ones that don't make a big fuss about it. In other words, the information about a condition is low key and incidental to the story. Here is another reason to constantly be on the look-out for how illustrators embed references to disability as part of a 'normal' world view. Some early years publishers, like *Child's Play,* are committed to doing this as part of their philosophy and regularly include children with hearing aids and walking frames along with some other recognisable characteristics in their books aimed at very young children. There has recently been pressure

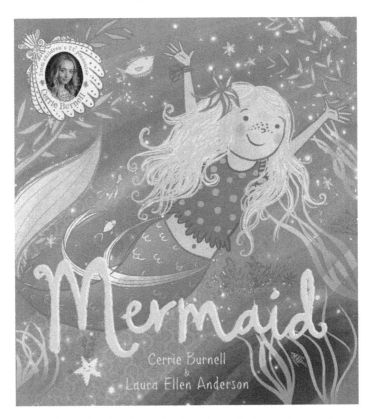

Figure 5.3 Example of a picture book with no disability clues on the cover. Burnell, C. (author) and Anderson, L. E. (illustrator). (2015)

on the publishing industry by campaigns like 'Everybody In' to stop them regarding portrayal of disability as a niche interest that isn't a viable commercial concern. They argue that, on the contrary, there is a huge untapped market of parents, carers and professionals who would love to see a better range that is easily available.

Mermaid by Cerrie Burrell, illustrated by Laura Ellen Anderson

This book is written by the TV presenter, Cerrie Burrell, who famously experienced hostile reactions from some parents on social media when she first appeared on a CBeebies programme because she has one fore-shortened arm. These parents seemed to be worried that her physical appearance might frighten their children and the furious backlash that followed which challenged these concerns is a very good example of why seeing disability in the mainstream media can help to shape attitudes. Here she has written a charming story about a little boy called Luka who lives by the sea with his family, none of whom can swim, although he is the only one that seems to mind. One day he sees a little girl swimming in the sea and watches as she is then lifted out by her dad who helps her into her wheelchair, which has beautifully decorated wheels. Her name is Sylvia, they become friends and she succeeds in teaching him how to swim. After they have said their goodbyes he has a vivid dream that she is really a mermaid and he is delighted to find that she is a new member of his class when he goes to school the next day. The last part of the story hints that he will help her to fit into her new environment to repay her for helping him to be confident in the sea. I really like this picture book because it emphasises how a child can help another to cope with unfamiliar challenges. It also gives the strong message that friendship is a key to adventures and imagination and that children with SEND are as complex and multi-talented as any other child.

These recommended books are not all easily available from mainstream suppliers but specialist distributors like Letterbox Library always carry a good variety with a disability-related theme. With a little online research, it is also possible to locate recommended book lists from BookTrust and many disability organisations. For instance, several years ago the charity Scope hosted a 3-year lottery funded project 'In the Picture' that looked at the dearth and limited availability of such picture books, and the list of recommended picture books that emerged as a result is still available. Specialist organisations like Outside In World provide lists and information about children's books from all over the world and these include some wonderful examples of picture books with disability-related content. The campaigning organisation Inclusive Minds and specialist book initiatives like The Letterpress Project also include a wealth of reviews of recommended inclusive books.

Beyond picture books: imaginative and small world play

Any imaginative play area should include a wide range of resources that reflect the real world and these could include items like walking frames, spectacles and other adaptive equipment. The role of the adult is significant here because some intervention can help to create scenarios either inspired by the real world, or by stories that help the children to think about potential difficulties and barriers. This is also a way of developing and encouraging empathy as well as recognising different skills and expertise. Although hospital role play might be seen as one obvious area in which to do this, it is important that this isn't the only occasion that it happens because people with SEND may experience some ongoing medical interventions but rarely go to hospital for a cure.

There have been a few small world figures and dolls available for quite some time through mainstream educational resources providers and there is really no excuse for not at least having a wheelchair user included in resources. More recently there has been some campaigning by disability groups for big well-known manufacturers to improve their range of figures with some positive results. There are now dolls with a range of physical disabilities available from some educational and specialist providers, including some with prosthetic limbs and guide dogs to support visually and hearing-impaired people. The commercially produced 'Persona dolls' are often recommended as useful early years resources because they include a series of individual characters, some of which have SEND. However, these are quite expensive and in the past, with the sewing skills of talented parents, I have created more rough and ready bespoke dolls that can be used to equally good effect.

Displays, posters and anything else

An effective inclusive early years curriculum relies on practitioners who use imagination and creativity alongside the provision of specific resources. Even very young children will respond to challenges in their play and this also encourages problem-solving and creative skills plus collaborative working. With the support of an adult or 'knowledgeable other' they will be encouraged to think about the benefits of an inclusive society by recognising and doing something about potential barriers in line with the social model approach.

Example

Resources in the wet sand play: farm buildings; a range of construction materials including wooden bricks and Duplo; farm animals; a range of small world figures; easy access to paper and card; felt pens; scissors; sellotape.

Challenge: some children are coming to visit the farm including Fatima who is a wheelchair user, Poppy who has a walking frame, Jamal who is visually impaired, Marlon who has sickle cell anaemia and Danny who has ASD (use appropriate terminology according to the age and the experience of the children). Help the farmer to make sure that everyone sees all the animals and has a lovely time.

Things to think about

- How will Fatima and Poppy travel over the sand? Perhaps make a smoother path using flat wooden bricks and ramps where necessary.

- How will Jamal be able to find his way along the path and read the signs? Ideas might include making signs on fluorescent paper.

- What happens if Marlon feels tired or Danny needs somewhere quiet to sit? Perhaps add some chairs and a sheltered space constructed with Duplo and a paper canopy.

The key to supporting any imaginative play is practitioner knowledge and appropriate preparation so that the children can begin to anticipate what might need to happen. Perhaps a told story with props beforehand could introduce the premise and provide a narrative framework to build on later. The subsequent play should not be formulaic but different issues and opportunities might evolve, for example introduce one of the children's mums as a character who is worried and needs reassurance: 'What will happen if Jamal needs to rest?'.

The different stages of the story could be recorded with photographs and annotation added later to make a book or display. The example given could easily be adapted for other small world play, dolls and soft toys and role play in a range of scenarios.

Sometimes a picture book might provide inspiration for imaginative play. For example, *Rolling along with Goldilocks and the Three Bears* by Cindy Meyers, illustrated by Carol Morgan, includes Baby Bear as a wheelchair user and this means that other small changes need to happen in the story in terms of the environment. This really gets children problem solving as well as beginning to have some understanding of the everyday barriers for wheelchair users. This story could easily be acted out using teddy bears of varying sizes with all the usual props for the traditional story plus a toy wheelchair and adapted bed.

The wider physical environment sends strong messages about the overall ethos of an early years setting. It is very important to convey that children and people with SEND are part of the landscape by selecting posters and other information that show this. Many settings use photographs of their own children and families to do this but this might only include a few (if any) people with SEND. So it is good to know that these can be easily supplemented with some excellent reasonably priced resources available from organisations like Kids Like Me.

High-quality early years practice is inclusive – it is not an optional 'add-on'. However, being a reflective inclusive early years practitioner means being able to recognise the gaps in personal and professional knowledge, and then to do something about it. This includes being prepared to find out how and where to locate resources including picture books, and this is a good excuse to spend time looking at books in the local children's library and bookshops where knowledgeable staff will always be glad to give advice. Books can be quite expensive so it is also a good idea to regularly browse charity and remainder shops for some excellent bargains. Provision of a good range is vital but most significant is to be able to then use these effectively with children. Picture books are very powerful cultural artefacts, particularly those aimed at younger readers as they contribute to shaping their initial view of the world. Only through experiencing a wide variety of such books might they (and adult readers) begin to fully understand the important message about ordinariness alongside the 'specialness' of such children.

Conclusion

In summary, an early years setting that is packed with the latest expensive equipment and picture books that reflect positive images is most influential if these are used by well-informed and confident staff who all understand their potential value in contributing to a better understanding of SEND, and that are made available to all children on a regular basis.

Further reading

Graham, J. (2008) Picture books: Looking Closely in Goodwin, P. (ed.) *Understanding Children's Books: a guide for education professionals.* London: Sage Publications Ltd.

Saunders, K. (2000) *Happy Ever Afters: a storybook code to teaching children about disability.* Stoke on Trent: Trentham Books Ltd.

Whitehead, M. (2010) *Language and Literacy in the Early Years 0-7,* 4th edition, London: Sage Publications Ltd.

Supporting communication

Chris Collett

This chapter will:

- discuss the centrality of speech, language and communication to young children's development

- explore the nature of speech, language and communication needs, with reference to specific difficulties in communication that can arise

- consider a range of strategies that will maximise communication opportunities for all children, whilst supporting those with SLCN

- discuss alternative and augmentative communication systems that can support specific communication needs

Importance of speech, language and communication

> *Communication is the number one skill. Without it, children will struggle to make friends, learn and enjoy life.*
>
> (Talking Point 2016)

It has long been recognised that speech, language and communication hold the key to success. Communication is inextricably linked to children's development, to their well-being and, in our society, to their self-determination (making decisions about what happens in their own lives), and consequently to their life opportunities. Bercow (2008:3) recognised the fundamental importance of speech, language and communication, describing it as a 'precious commodity'.

Communication is intrinsically linked to children's ability to make their needs known and to assert their rights. Speech and language systems allow children to organise their thoughts, classify and store information (Tassoni 2015). Through internalising language systems, children develop abstract concepts and thoughts, such as understanding time; past, present and future. They use language for thinking; to imagine and recreate roles and experiences; to clarify ideas or refer to events they have observed or are curious about, and to problem solve, all of which helps them to make sense of the world. Communication and interaction with others enables children to develop social relationships and express their thoughts and feelings, and is linked to emotional well-being and sound mental health. There are obvious links to literacy and learning, which are central to the industrialised world, and children who struggle to communicate will struggle with these things too.

The early years is a crucial time for learning to communicate and usually the time when the dramatic shift from non-verbal to verbal language occurs. It is also the time when young children are developing their sense of self, developing independence, and learning that through communication, they can have some measure of control over their environment. In order to support all these things, the practitioner must develop strategies for understanding and supporting children who may communicate differently.

But the centrality of communication is more than simply a personal statement of value. UNICEF, UNESCO and the World Health Organization list communication as one of the ten core life skills and a fundamental human right. Since the 1989 United Nations Convention on the Rights of the Child (UNICEF 1989), there has been a growing understanding of the necessity for children themselves to express their views when decisions are being made about their lives, as part of developing self-determination. The 2015 SEND Code of Practice makes it clear that the child or young person should *participate as fully as possible* in, for example, the development of a personalised plan, an EHC and when decisions about educational placement are made. Many children, especially as they get older, will be able to communicate their views by simply telling an adult. For very young, or developmentally young, children this may not be so immediately straightforward, but the responsibility nonetheless lies with the adults involved, to ensure that the child's wishes are recorded and taken into account.

Speech, language and communication needs

In understanding the value of speech, language and communication it is perhaps easier to consider the effects when these skills, that many of us take for granted, are absent.

> I can remember the frustration of not being able to talk. I knew what I wanted to say, but I could not get the words out, so I would just scream.
>
> (Grandin 2016)

According to Afasic (2008) one in ten children in the UK or two to three in every classroom will have communication difficulties that require specialist help, and more than 20 per cent of EHCRs (formerly statements of SEN), for primary-age children, include provision to support speech and language difficulties. At least 1 in 500 children will have a persistent long-term speech and language impairment that needs particular specialist support. Bercow (2008) describes SLCN as a 'profoundly damaging disability'. Children and young people who have speech, language and communication needs (SLCN) commonly have difficulties with reading and writing and accessing the curriculum. They also often have poor behaviour and may find it hard to socialise with their peers. Poor speech, language and communication have additionally been linked to social exclusion (ICan 2009).

There are two groups of children with speech, language and communication needs. Those whose SLCN are their primary need, and children with other special educational needs and disabilities, who will often experience associated SLCN. Children who have SEND may be delayed at any stage of the process of developing speech, language and communication. Children who remain developmentally young may not progress beyond pre-intentional communication, meaning that it is the adult's responsibility to interpret their behaviour, in order to understand and meet their needs. Other children may find communication challenging due to other impairments or conditions, for example autism, learning disability, hearing impairment or cerebral palsy. These children may have unusual or disordered speech, language and communication and will need specific interventions to reach their full potential (ICan 2016).

Other children may have a specific speech, language and communication need, such as a cleft palate or aphasia. Their difficulties may be with receptive language (understanding), which may then impact on their ability to express themselves. Or they may have a specific expressive language (speaking) difficulty. Children may have difficulty with the 'mechanics' of listening and speaking, or they may have difficulty understanding the rules and functions of spoken language or 'how it works'.

Typically, 3-year-olds should be able to produce clear words and string them together into short sentences, tell simple stories, understand instructions and interpret others' non-verbal communication. Researchers broadly agree that while there is an innate tendency for language to develop, the frequency and quality of interactions between child and adult, and an environment to support communication, are also crucial. For some years now there have been widespread concerns about the low status of talk and interaction, as they increasingly compete with other aspects of modern living, such as TV, computers and tablets. There may also be children, often (though not always) in areas of social disadvantage, who may have had limited language experience and therefore come into the setting with delayed communication skills. These children may find it hard to listen and have a poor vocabulary and immature speech patterns. There are implications too for the development of heathy attachments and social/emotional skills and concerns that engaging with electronic visual media can foster passivity and a lack of social engagement. Children are therefore arriving in early years settings without the required tools to successfully interact with others and build relationships. A study by Locke, Ginsborg and Peers (2002) identified direct links between SCLN and socio-economic status, but Bercow (2008:14) rightly warns against making assumptions about children from particular backgrounds. And with the right support early on, these children will have the potential to catch up with their peers.

Specific SLC needs

As with all special needs and disabilities, there is a continuum; from children who have mild difficulties that can be easily resolved through differentiated activities, to children with complex and profound needs who will need high levels of support throughout their lives. Within this range are a number of specific identifiable conditions that will have an effect on speech, language and communication.

Aphasia/dysphasia: you may come across these terms, which historically have been used in the field of specific language impairments; aphasia, meaning no speech and dysphasia, meaning poor speech. These terms are still widely used to describe adults with acquired language difficulties. Dysphasia may still be used to describe a child who struggles with speech and language, but it is more common these days in the UK to say that a child has speech, language and communication needs (SLCN).

Auditory processing: understanding what is said to us means hearing spoken language, then 'decoding' and interpreting it, in the part of the brain that deals with language. To follow instructions or participate in conversations this process needs to work efficiently and in a fraction of a second. Some children may have a breakdown in this processing.

Difficulty with articulation and fluency (sometimes called dysfluency): when speaking, a child may find it difficult to link together sounds or words and phrases as a continuous flow. Many children as they are learning the complexities of language, alongside learning to speak, may stammer or stutter on particular sounds, or at the beginning of words or phrases.

Phonology: a child may have difficulty with discriminating, or reproducing accurately, the different sounds that make up words.

Prosody (intonation and stress): the child may not hear, understand or be able to replicate the different emphases placed on words or phrases that we use to help convey meaning, for example 'I went *to* the park', instead of 'I went to the *park*'.

Semantics (the meaning of words/phrases): the child may be able to imitate and recite long and complex sentences, but without understanding what the words and phrases mean. For example, a child may learn 'parrot-fashion' a whole story that is frequently read to them, or the dialogue in a film or TV show, without understanding anything about what happens in the story.

Pragmatics: again, a child may appear to have a good grasp of quite complex language, but fails to understand how and why language is used socially. Temple Grandin, a woman with autism, has famously said that, even as a highly successful adult, she continues to have difficulty understanding the turn taking, give and take involved in conversation, and will often interrupt inappropriately (Webb 1992).

Syntax: the child may find it difficult to grasp the grammatical rules of language, for example tenses and plurals, so that language remains immature, for example: 'I runned'.

Selective talking or mutism: even though the child is competent in spoken language, he or she may decline to speak in certain circumstances, for example, in the setting. This can persist over weeks and months, sometimes years, and can be frustrating, especially if the child 'chooses' not to speak in the setting, but at home time can be heard chatting fluently to parents or carers who collect them. There is often an underlying psychological cause, so it is important to seek specialist help and to ensure that the child is given strategies to communicate through other means, without being put under pressure to speak.

It should be remembered that *all* children may experience some, or all, of the above as a short-term developmental phase, while they are getting to grips with the complexities of spoken language. Instead of drawing too much attention to these irregularities, practitioners should support the child's efforts by modelling the 'correct' version clearly and consistently, and providing alternative means of communication where needed (see below). Language used by the adult should be appropriate to the child's level of understanding. For a few children, difficulties may persist over a much longer period or permanently. These children will need careful and sensitive interventions to overcome the difficulty, and/ or alternative strategies that will help them to communicate effectively.

Overlapping conditions that may impact on communication skills

Dyspraxia or developmental coordination disorder (DCD): describes an impairment or immaturity of the organisation of thought and movement. This means that the child will struggle to make the link between ideation (thinking what to do), planning how to do it and execution of the task. Again, this is a thought process that we take for granted; for most people it happens automatically and within a split second.

Figure 6.1 Ideation, planning and execution

As Figure 6.1 suggests, this condition impacts on a child's ability to process and act on information in a coordinated way, and often presents difficulties with 'daily living' activities, such as feeding, dressing, reading and writing. It affects both large and small movements, including the coordination of the oral muscles – jaw, lips and tongue – and thus can lead to delayed speech, language and communication skills. DCD affects approximately one in ten children (so in a class of 30, at least one child is likely to have DCD), and boys are affected more frequently than girls.

Cerebral palsy (CP): 'a permanent but non-progressive disorder of posture and movement, resulting from damage to the developing brain, during pregnancy, delivery, or the first two years' (Bax 1964). CP is caused by damage to the brain that then interferes with the neurological signals sent to the muscles. The condition can be mild or severe and can affect children's physical skills in a number of ways. Muscles may have low tone, meaning that the child will be very 'floppy', or high tone, which causes muscles to tighten and restrict movement. Again, the oral muscles are also often affected, which will impact on the child's ability to develop spoken language, and damage to the area of the brain responsible for communication may also lead to difficulties with processing language. But it is important to remember that the child's cognitive skills may not be affected.

Hearing impairment (including glue ear): children learn much of their spoken language through hearing and imitating those around them, which is an almost continual process. They are hearing words, phrases and sentences many times over and in varying contexts, so can learn, generalise and consolidate their understanding. The effect of a hearing impairment on that learning should not be underestimated, both in terms of language learning, and also the impact on the understanding of abstract concepts that are language-dependent, as discussed above.

Autism spectrum disorder: in recent years, there has been an explosion in the number of children diagnosed with ASD, but

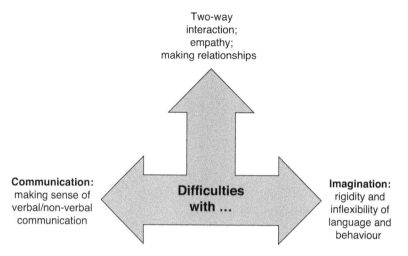

Figure 6.2 Triad of impairment. An adaption of Wing and Gould 1979

along with it, understanding has also grown. Beside some more recently recognised characteristics, ASD means that a child will have difficulty with communication, social interaction and flexibility of thought and behaviour, as illustrated by Wing's 'Triad of Impairment' (Figure 6.2). Approximately 1 in 100 children in the UK have the condition (NAS 2017), and again, more boys than girls are affected. Though the general rule is that children are diagnosed at around 30 months, some children might present with these difficulties from much earlier, and some early diagnosis (by medical professionals) does occur.

In terms of communication, practitioners might notice: the use of echolalia (echoing rather than responding to speech); unusual intonation, or emphasis on words (see also prosody above); the repeated use of 'stereotyped' or learned phrases; a literal understanding and use of language – phrases such as 'I died laughing' can be very confusing and even upsetting for a child with ASD; and a functional use of language only, that is, purely as a means to having needs met. If under pressure, a child who is verbal may also have a 'communication breakdown', lapsing into an endless, intense monologue, perhaps as part of a tantrum.

A child with ASD will also struggle to interact with others, failing to recognise or understand the more subtle aspects of communication: non-verbal signals of facial expression, gesture and body language. Social timing, for example in two-way conversations, may also be poor, and although the child may respond to social interaction it is unlikely that s/he will initiate.

What does all this mean?

The implications for all of the above difficulties described, are that a child may struggle with:

- listening and attention
- discriminating sounds
- recognising sequences or patterns
- picking out key information
- cognitive processing and organising thoughts
- memory; word finding or retrieval
- social interaction.

Barriers to early identification

Where other additional needs may be quite easily identified, language difficulties, especially in young children, can be more problematic. Many practitioners are, quite rightly, reluctant to 'label' children too soon, when the difficulties being experienced may be due to lack of experience or immaturity. And whilst practitioners are clear on the approximate ages when children would be expected to reach physical milestones, such as sitting or walking, there can be wider variation in the age and the manner in which children acquire language. The subtleties of some SLCN may not be apparent at an early age, and young children are often quick to adapt, appearing to cope with familiar people, routines and situations, and so masking any language difficulty.

I would reiterate that it is important also to be aware – without making assumptions – of children's language experiences and opportunities before coming into the setting. This will include knowing about the family dynamics. Children with older siblings may have delayed language acquisition because others speak for them, or because their needs are met automatically, so they do not have to make them known. Parents may sometimes also cite examples of other family members who were 'late talkers', which can be valid, but should not be relied on as evidence that the child will inevitably 'catch up'.

English as an additional language (EAL)

In these days of mass migration, some children may well come into the setting with little or no English. However, not speaking English is not the same as not developing spoken language and it's important to differentiate between children who have limited English, but are acquiring their home language age appropriately, and children who have genuine difficulties with acquiring *any* spoken language. Children's home languages should be valued; many children who have English as an additional language (EAL) will pick up English relatively quickly and easily, but it's important to be alert to the fact that EAL can sometimes mask genuine difficulties. Similarly, children who are prone to common ear, nose and throat conditions, such as glue ear, may also be concealing more serious underlying difficulties with communication.

Identification and intervention

Communication and language development involves giving children opportunities to experience a rich language environment; to develop their confidence and skills in expressing themselves; and to speak and listen in a range of situations.

(DfE 2012)

Pre-verbal, verbal and non-verbal communication

As an Area SENCo and latterly as a lecturer on Early Years BA and Foundation Degree programmes, I would sometimes hear a practitioner say that a child was 'unable to communicate' due to his/her disabilities. What they meant of course, was that due to a child's particular needs, it was difficult to understand *what* the child was communicating. All children begin to communicate from the moment they are born, either with or without intending to.

Pre-intentional communication

For the first days and weeks of life, communication will not be intentional or purposeful, but a new born baby will give off signals, through body language and sounds, to indicate when s/he is hungry, tired or uncomfortable. It is then the job of the adult to interpret and respond to those basic indications of need. It is possible that a child with profound and complex needs may not move on from this stage of communication for a very long time, if at all. In such an instance, it may also be that the signals given off by the child are not obvious and do not conform to our expectations: for example, a child may make a wailing sound to indicate that s/he is happy, even though the sound suggests that they might be sad or in distress. The key to making sense of what a child with such profound needs might be communicating, is to talk to parents and family members, who will have come to recognise even the subtlest of signals. It is then vital to observe and record in detail the child's responses and behaviour in a range of different situations, so that his/her communication signals can be shared with, and understood by, all staff in the setting. This may sound quite a passive approach, but the aim in doing this is to begin to move towards establishing two-way communication and interaction with the child (see also Chapter 7). And of course, it should never be assumed that the child who is non-verbal (unable to speak) has nothing to say.

Intentional communication

As they grow and develop, most children, over time, will begin to communicate intentionally with the people around them. The first step in this process is to establish eye contact with another person. This immediately engages that other person in eliciting a response, to have needs met or to simply share an experience. This is also known as 'shared attention'. Once the child has made eye contact, he or she can then communicate simple needs and desires by shifting his/her gaze to an object, picture or symbol using eye-pointing or eye gaze. The child can then make choices and express preferences, beginning with a simple choice between two items and gradually increasing to a wider range. For children with developmental delay, who continue to use this as their primary mode of communication, there are some simple commercially produced devices that can support this process, such as the 'Eye-Tran' (eye transfer frame), which allows the child to choose from up to four different options (Martin-Denham 2015:96). The majority of children, however, will move on from this stage and their mode of communication (way of communicating) will become more sophisticated and effective as they progress into understanding and then using symbolic language (words) to communicate verbally.

For children who have visual impairment, clearly there must be an alternative way of establishing this contact, or shared attention, and initially this will be through touch and the use of real objects, or 'objects of reference', but the practitioner will need to also be aware of a child who doesn't enjoy touch and who may be tactile defensive. This child may need to go through a desensitisation process before interaction can be attempted (see Chapter 7). Similarly, while establishing eye contact might be the primary aim for many children with complex needs, there are some children on the autism spectrum who will find this in itself a challenge. Instead, early simple two-way interaction is indicated by the child showing, through their body language, an awareness of the other person, and that they are awaiting a response. Parents of children with ASD also often report that their child did not 'share attention' as a baby or toddler, which reflects the child's lack of understanding of communication as a social experience.

General strategies

Whatever the child's specific needs might be in terms of SLCN, there are a number of general strategies that will help. To facilitate young children's understanding, it is important to have a clear, consistent and effective means of communication using language appropriate to the child's level of understanding, which may mean using simple language and key words. This can feel unnatural and even disrespectful, as we are accustomed to providing children with a rich language environment that uses complex phrases and sentences. But for children who struggle to understand and process spoken language, it is necessary to give them only the information they need to make sense of a situation and know what to do. When giving instructions, it's also important to start with the child's name, to get his/her attention.

For example, if you would like Ellie to put on her coat and go outside, the only words needed are: *Ellie, coat, outside*. It is likely that Ellie will also be helped by some contextual clues. She will know what she is expected to do with her coat, may recognise the familiar routine for the time of day, and will see the behaviour of the other children. Chunking information might also help, so the instructions might be delivered in stages: 1) *Ellie, coat.* 2) *Ellie, coat on.* 3) *Ellie, outside.* Try to always give information too about what *should* be done. Children often only hear/remember the last couple of words spoken to them so if they are told 'please don't throw the sand' they will hear '–throw the sand' and do the opposite of what is expected!

Having been given an instruction, the child may then need to be allowed time to process what s/he has heard – it may be up to about 10 seconds before a child responds. Gestural clues and visual clues, such as objects and pictures, may also help to 'scaffold' the child's understanding and/or expression. Tassoni (2015:126) wisely advises that practitioners should be language *partners* rather than *teachers*, and certainly it is important to not ask too many direct questions or put pressure on children to speak, especially when there is a communication difficulty. This approach can make interaction seem confrontational and challenging. Instead, practitioners need to create comfortable opportunities for communication and interaction. Stories, rhymes and

songs encourage communication but in a way that is enjoyable, especially where there is repetition and an opportunity for children to 'fill
the gaps'. In addition, any activity can be made 'language rich' through
providing a simple commentary that introduces and reinforces new
words, for example: *I see you're putting the bricks together to make a
big tower.* Interaction can also be prompted by practitioners making
deliberate mistakes or 'sabotaging' activities, for example saying one
thing but doing another, or having missing or wrong equipment for
an activity. If you sit down to read a story, but say: *Today I'm going to
read this banana,* most children will react spontaneously. Changing
the environment – especially in a way that doesn't immediately make
sense – can have the same effect. Tassoni (2015:134–7) suggests some
further basic activities that can be tried.

Speech and language therapy

Where a child's communication difficulties are significant, it will be
necessary to make a referral to a speech and language therapist for
more specific targeted interventions and advice. In these instances,
crucial factors are:

- early identification and intervention;
- a continuum of services designed around the family;
- effective joint working.

Augmentative and alternative communication (AAC)

For some children who find traditional forms of communication difficult, it will be helpful to provide tools that will either support (aug-
ment) their development of spoken language, or replace it with an
alternative mode of communication. Children who have a significant
hearing impairment may well be introduced to British Sign Language
(BSL) by their teacher of the deaf. Children whose speech and language

is delayed still have a need to be able to communicate, but may have difficulties with listening and/or auditory processing, so visual clues, such as objects, pictures/photographs and symbols will be helpful.

Picture exchange communication system or PECS®

Probably the visual system most commonly used in settings is PECS®, which was developed in 1985 by Bondy and Frost. It uses pictures or symbols (whichever is appropriate) to teach children, in the first instance, the function or purpose of communication. The child is taught to give the picture of a desired item to a 'communicative partner', who immediately responds by giving the child (in exchange) that desired item. Thus, the child learns that if s/he communicates a need, that need will be addressed. From this simple transaction, the child can begin to build a pictorial vocabulary, discriminate between different objects and actions and eventually go on to communicate in more complex phrases and sentences. The success of PECS® is largely due to its simplicity and flexibility; resources can easily be made and accessed, and the principles can be applied in any situation that is relevant to the child.

Makaton® and baby signing

Makaton® is a system of gestural signing designed to support the language development of young, or developmentally young children. It differs from British Sign Language in that it is not designed to be used instead of spoken language, but is used in conjunction with it, so that children are encouraged to sign the word, but also say it at the same time. And whereas BSL has all the facets of grammatical structure, Makaton is deliberately restricted to the key essential words and vocabulary that children and young people may need to communicate their needs and wishes. The aim is that when children begin to develop verbal communication naturally, then Makaton® will cease to be needed, but it is also accepted that some children and young people will need to use Makaton® in the long term. As with PECS®, Makaton® is flexible and can be tailored to a child's individual needs. Makaton® picture symbols can also be used to enable the child to communicate at a more complex level:

- sharing thoughts, choices and emotions;
- taking part in games and activities;
- listening to, reading and telling stories.

Baby signing, 'Sing and Sign' or 'Singalong' are simplified versions of Makaton® that can be used for babies and toddlers who are developing early communication. They are generally used in conjunction with songs and rhymes.

Case study 6.1: Shanila

Shanila is three and a half and has recently begun attending a day nursery full time. She is a happy, playful child who loves to be outside, running about or climbing, and using the slide. She also enjoys chasing games with the other children and often pretends to be a monster, roaring at them. When they pretend to be afraid and run away, Shanila laughs and repeats the game. When she is inside, Shanila often chooses to play in the home corner. She dresses up, puts lots of the toys in her bag and walks around the nursery, babbling and singing to herself, though no clear words are discernible.

Shanila chooses from the whole range of toys available, usually preferring to play alone, but she willingly comes to staff-directed activities, and seems to enjoy the adult attention. She often seems to watch what the other children are doing and copies them when making, for example, a collage. However, she will only join in these more structured activities when an adult is present at the table. Shanila is always proud of anything she has made and is excited about showing it to her mum.

Shanila can say *mama* but has no other recognisable words, though she babbles with conversational intonation. Shanila's mum feels that her daughter is very bright and 'understands everything'. When Shanila wants something at home she can usually find and get it for herself; and when it is time to go out, Shanila gets her own shoes and coat, ready for her mum to help her put them on.

- What further background information would help you to make an accurate assessment of Shanila's speech, language and communication needs?

- What strategies could be implemented to support Shanila?

Wider support

In 2009, the Bercow Report (2008:59) identified a support system for SLCN that was 'characterised by high variability and a lack of equity'. In order to address these shortcomings, a number of recommendations were made and these have met with varying success. Some, such as the requirement for local authorities to provide information for parents, have been incorporated into the 2014 Children and Families Act. The Communication Council has since become the Communication Trust, which continues to promote SLC. Other recommendations, such as the appointment of a Communication Champion, have been more short-lived. The post, given to Jean Gross in 2010, was intended to run until March 2012, but the end date was later revised to December 2011, and the role has now become defunct. There is however a planned review of the outcomes of the report, and 'Bercow – Ten Years On' will be published in early 2018 (ICan 2016).

The Rose Review (2009) went on to make explicit links between speaking and listening and literacy. This has prompted a focus in early reading on the synthetic phonics approach. For obvious reasons, many of which are described above, this exclusive focus – reliant on the discrimination of letter sounds – is not suitable for many children with SLCN. The recently introduced phonics testing for young children also disadvantages those with particular SLCN. It can only be hoped that creative practitioners, and eventually policy-makers, recognise the value and importance of multi-method approaches to the teaching of reading.

Conclusion

Speech, language and communication are the most important skills young children will acquire. They underpin cognitive and social development and provide the mechanism by which children can make their needs, wishes and views known and move towards independence and self-determination. It is the responsibility of practitioners to ensure that children with SLCN are effectively supported to develop communication skills, or are given an alternative means of communicating with those around them.

Further reading

Brown, S. (2015) *Autism Spectrum Disorder & De-escalation Strategies. A practical guide to positive behavioural interventions for children and young people.* London: Jessica Kingsley Publishers.

Farrell, M. (2008) *Educating Special Children.* Abingdon: David Fulton.

Multisensory approaches to learning

Ingrid Smith

This chapter will:

- explain what is meant by multisensory learning, and why a multi-sensory approach is central to working with children with complex physical, cognitive and sensory needs

- detail how to plan meaningful activities for children with complex physical, cognitive and sensory needs, based on sensory experiences

- give examples of how stories and other activities can be developed into multisensory learning experiences for children

- discuss the use of everyday objects and materials in creating multi-sensory spaces, using both indoor and outdoor environments

As a newly qualified practitioner back in the early 1980s, working in special schools, it quickly became apparent to me that not all the children I worked with were able to access the teaching and learning opportunities I had created. In those days, we only had access to basic medical information about the children we worked with, so unless a child had clearly recognisable needs, or had been prescribed glasses or hearing aids, we were left to discover their sensory functioning by observation and trial and error. Information about different learning styles was in its infancy, and computers had yet to be invented.

In those days, there were no interactive whiteboards, tablets or lap-tops to create stimulating learning opportunities. Classroom budgets were nonexistent and educational catalogues contained only the basic resources suitable for children whose development was within 'normal' limits. But unfettered by a prescriptive curriculum, what we did have was the luxury of being able to try out the different ideas we had dreamed up, or had read about in books. I quickly developed a habit of collecting ordinary everyday materials (what some might call rubbish!), by visiting charity shops and car boot sales. This enabled me to build an extensive bank of resources that could be used in the classroom.

There are five main senses through which we take in information and learn about the world around us. Babies begin to do this from the moment they are born and latest research would indicate that this process begins even earlier, while the baby is still in the womb.

Sight (the visual sense): provides us with the quickest way to investigate and understand what is happening in our immediate environment. Information in the form of images enters though the eye, travels along the optic nerve and is then interpreted by the brain. Each image in turn is processed to inform us: how near or far away something is, its depth, its colour, its shades, its contrast, its lighting, whether it has fine details and whether the item is a whole or a part of something larger.

Hearing (the auditory sense): is closely related to vision. We use our eyes and ears together to locate sounds; we actively turn our heads to track the sound and then use our vision to interpret the integrated image of what we see.

Smell (the olfactory sense): is very closely linked to taste, enabling us to determine, among other things, what is safe to eat, and what isn't. Smell is also connected with our emotions, and is potent in creating and recreating memories – the smell of newly cut grass might be a reminder of a picnic, or school sports day or simply that summer is coming.

Taste (the gustatory sense): is about flavours and also the textures of what we eat. It is closely related to smell, and if we lose the sense of smell, we also lose our sense of taste.

Touch (the tactile sense): our skin is the largest sensory organ of all. It covers the whole of our body both inside and out. One of the most sensitive parts of our body is the hands. They can provide us with feedback about texture, outlines, pressure, weight, temperature, volume and movements, such as vibrations.

Today it is recognised that altogether we have between nine and twenty-one senses, the traditional five, above, plus the vestibular (balance), temperature (heat and cold), pain, proprioception (awareness of our own body in space) and many others.

Multisensory: means using two or more senses together.

We learn about the world around us through using our senses to help us to interact meaningfully with it. Babies and children explore and play in different environments; they learn that some objects can be eaten and others can't; some smell nice and others unpleasant, some may hurt us and others feel nice, some make sounds and others are silent when shaken. This learning is ongoing throughout our lives; every experience we have adds more information to the fantastic encyclopedia which is our brain.

Example: the importance of sensory information and processing

Most of us give little thought to the underlying learning that has previously taken place before we go shopping; we look at our shopping list and read, for example, that we need a loaf of bread.

We enter the bread aisle in the supermarket, and even though we are faced with a huge range of choices, we know that all the different varieties of wrapped, unwrapped, sizes, shapes, colours and textures we can see are all still bread. How do we know this? Our brain is able to retrieve all the prior memories we have laid down about bread, using our sensory systems.

Our *sight* has enabled the brain to develop and store visual memories of all the varieties of bread we have seen, enabling us to identify each shape, colour and texture and know that although each is different, it is still bread. Our sense of *smell* has enabled the brain to retain and recall the smell of bread. Our *hearing* has enabled the brain to retain the memory of the sounds made when we bite into and chew a slice of bread or a bread roll. Our sense of *taste*, has been able to develop memories of how different breads, sliced white bread, rye bread and granary bread, taste. Our *touch* system has enabled the brain to develop memories about the texture, weight, shape and firmness of the different bread types. The *vestibular* and *proprioceptive* systems (movement) enable us to recall picking up a loaf of bread from the shelf, how heavy it will be, and how much 'force' we need to pick it up.

The brain requires more information than just the image of a loaf of bread to inform us that what we see is bread; it requires a total integrated package of information, from all these senses combined, to develop a full understanding of what we see. It is only when all our senses are engaged that we can learn and retain information. Indeed, how many of us have flashbacks of memories when we hear a particular sound or experience a smell, such as the sound of a drill and the smell of antiseptic mouthwash that take us (perhaps unwillingly!) back to the dentist's surgery?

What we know about learning styles is linked to our understanding of the senses. We know there are three main learning styles, visual, auditory and kinaesthetic, each of which requires a different teaching approach.

To enable children to develop fully we need to create curiosity in the classroom or setting, we need to capture children's interest and gain their attention and stimulate their senses. To ensure that all children's learning styles are catered for, sessions must be designed with visual and auditory stimuli for the first two types of learners and with practical hands-on activities for the kinaesthetic learners. As practitioners, we must create a safe environment. Children need to feel safe socially and emotionally and be able to make mistakes without censure. Only then are they able to participate fully and learn.

Multisensory learning and SEND

We can see how important sensory learning is for all children, but for children who have physical, sensory or intellectual difficulties and who are developmentally young, opportunities to explore and interact with the environment are often very different. Limitations of movement, vision, hearing, cognitive ability, behavioural difficulties, perception issues, pain and other problems create obstacles to their enjoyment of life and opportunities to engage.

To enable children with sensory and/or physical difficulties to access information, we need to look at all the activities within their daily lives and present them in a sensory-focused way. Activities must have meaning for these children and allow them to experience and develop an understanding of cues which enable them to make predictions and build up that 'backstory' of experiences which allows them to make sense of the world around them. We need to provide environments where they have opportunities to use various senses to stimulate the whole sensory system.

Self-engagement behaviours

Many children with sensory disabilities also engage in what are termed self-engagement behaviours. They may rock, make noises or display other behaviours which they use to stimulate themselves, often to compensate for reduced sensory input from their immediate environment. The job of the practitioner is to help these children to develop more beneficial person or object engagement behaviours. We need to teach them that interacting with an adult is safe and fun and that toys and other stimuli are more rewarding than being passive or engaging in self-stimulation.

Children who avoid physical stimuli

When we look around our settings we may see some children who also avoid stimuli. They may be passive and non-responsive; they may pull away or they may physically remove themselves from the activity or group. Other children may be hyperactive so they don't actually pay attention to the activity or the adult. As practitioners, we need to support these children to become aware of their surroundings and develop an understanding that a world exists outside themselves. To do this, we need to begin with activities that are non-threatening and do not involve touch. Traditionally, to gain children's attention and most importantly their trust, we have used bubbles, sounds and smells. Only when we have gained their trust can we move on to structured 'massage' activities which are used to 'desensitise' and develop physical trust. At this stage, stimuli are presented to a child to explore *by* an adult, rather than expecting the child to engage in active exploration independently.

Initially, to enable a child to explore, the adult may need to support the child with their exploration of their physical surroundings, objects and people, using modelling and in some instances, physical prompting, including hand-over-hand coactive methods. Hence, time is needed to allow the child to develop physical trust that will enable him or her to accept this close physical proximity. Through these activities the child can be supported to develop preferences, establish cause and effect relationships, object permanence and discrimination.

When we observe other children within the setting, we can see that they are no longer using trial and error techniques and are using all their senses to explore their surroundings and integrate experiences.

For children in early years settings working at a sensory level, it has briefly been mentioned that we should start with everyday activities and not take for granted that all the children have the same understanding and come to the setting having had the same experiences. To maximise participation during our planned sensory focused activities it is important to:

1. Analyse the task so that it is broken down into a small number of individual steps, ensuring the focus is on the sensory opportunities and not the end product (see also Chapter 2).

2. Make sure the steps are presented in a way which will stimulate the senses, that is, include materials to taste, smell, look at, listen to and feel.

3. Allow opportunities for the child to make and communicate choices.

4. Ensure that the children experience success; the activity presented needs to be appropriate to the child's skill levels.

5. Ensure that the child can actively join in as much as possible.

Turning everyday activities into multisensory experiences

When planning an activity or story with a sensory focus, I always talk myself through how I can ensure that *all* children will be able to access the concept I am trying to teach. I ask myself a number of questions:

- What prior knowledge or experience does each child bring to the activity?
- What, if any, sensory processing difficulties do they have?
- Do they have any physical limitations?
- Do they have cognitive (learning) disabilities?
- How do they communicate?
- Do they have a behaviour plan?
- Do they have any allergies?
- Are they able to tolerate oral consumption of food/drink?
- Are they able to sit and listen or do they prefer to be a 'hands-on' learner?

These questions enable me to create the optimum learning opportunities for all the children. For a child who has *visual* difficulties, I will need to know about the extent of these; is the child totally blind? Do they have a squint? Do they have tunnel or peripheral vision? Do they have cataracts? Do they have any functional vision? It may be necessary to provide extra lighting, or position the child so they are comfortable or that the light source, including sunlight, is directly behind them, falling over their shoulder onto the stimulus. I may need to move them closer to, for example, the interactive whiteboard or adult's face so they are able to 'see' what is happening and pick up on cues. The child may need his/her own resources to explore rather than looking at or sharing the group resource. The child may need longer to explore the materials using all his/her senses. Resources or materials may need to be larger or even smaller to enable the child to focus on the stimulus as a whole rather than just a part. The child may require additional magnification, or may just need to have their glasses cleaned!

Hearing-impaired children can be easily overlooked. Deafness is often regarded as the hidden disability as, unlike a visual or physical disability, it can't be seen. Very often, hearing-impaired children are thought of as challenging as they don't follow instructions. As practitioners, we may be the first to realise that the child may be experiencing hearing difficulties. Understanding hearing loss is difficult for those of us who have excellent hearing. What exactly does mild, moderate, profound, conductive or intermittent loss mean? This chapter does not propose to go into detail, but the child's Teacher of the Deaf (TOD) will be able to provide valuable information regarding the impact of the child's hearing loss. A rule of thumb is also that if a child has been prescribed hearing aids, it is imperative that they are in good working order and that the child wears them. Whilst independence with hearing aid management is always to be encouraged, with a younger child, parents may need to show practitioners how to change batteries, as they can run down. Spares should also be kept in the setting. Hearing aids with dead batteries are far worse than if the child wore no aids at all, as they effectively prevent any sound from entering the ear. It is also important for parents to show you how to put aids back together after a reluctant wearer has pulled them out and dismantled them! But it should be remembered that many hearing aids are not selective in the sounds they amplify; they amplify everything. Hence children who have never experienced hearing before may find it extremely uncomfortable or even frightening to be presented with this new sensation called sound.

With any hearing-impaired child, it is important to have information about their communication systems from parents or the TOD. Are they able to hear spoken language when aided? Can they lip read or do they require alternative communication methods, for example signing, pictures, symbols, communication books or objects of reference? It is important that all the adults working with the child are familiar with the system used, competent in its use and most importantly, consistent in using it. To not do so is denying the child equal access to learning opportunities. As with visually impaired children, light levels are important, so the child can see and consequently pick up on cues to help them understand what is required. Clear vision of the adult/person speaking to them is again essential to enable the child to observe lip patterns and facial expression. Sometimes it may be essential to attract the child's attention to inform them that their attention is required and enable them to look at the speaker.

A child may have *physical disabilities* which have an impact on their learning. He or she may find it difficult to move around the setting independently to take full advantage of the activities available. Mobility aids such as rolators or walking frames are cumbersome and may prevent the child from reaching equipment. For a younger child, a wheelchair will probably require an adult to push it. Often, even if the child is able to say where they want to go, the wheelchair will not be able to easily fit, for example, if the sand/water tray is too low. Many wheelchairs have trays that can be fitted to them, but activities are restricted to being in the chair and may prevent the child from easily interacting socially without careful intervention from adults. Many children with physical disabilities, especially those who have profound cerebral palsy may have limited head control which prevents them from observing what is happening. They may have no or limited movement in their arms which prevents them from reaching for and/or exploring objects without the intervention of an adult. Speech may be affected and augmentative communication systems may be required to enable the child to have a voice. Switches can be programmed to enable the child to answer 'yes' and 'no' questions, and to 'speak' during activities and to operate simple cause and effect toys. Many children with severe cerebral palsy are unable to drink or eat orally due to problems with breathing, which will curtail some learning opportunities available to them. In most instances, staff will be informed that a child is 'nil by mouth' before they enter the setting, but all practitioners need to be aware if this is the case. Similarly, it's important to know about any allergies a child might have; no-one wants to take a child to a hospital A&E department as the result of a 'fun' activity!

Staffing

The greatest tool to support children with profound and complex needs to make the most of learning opportunities, is our observational skills. The more we know about the children we work with, the easier it is to plan differentiated activities which will engage the children and motivate them to become independent, rather than passive learners.

Once the physical environment has been considered, the next step is to think about the adult support the child may need. Does the child have the cognitive or physical abilities to explore the resources independently or will they require the support of an adult? If this is necessary, the supporting adult needs to be as informed as possible about how much help the child needs. Too little help and the child will be unable to access the activity; too much and the child will experience the activity from a distance instead of participating and being an active learner. For example, the supporting adult needs to know that the child may not look directly at them or at objects, due to difficulties with turning their head; if the child understands spoken language, or uses an alternative communication system; and whether the child has an additional sensory disability, such as a hearing impairment.

So how does this look in practice?

Example one: planning a sensory story

To support the children's understanding of a traditional tale, I make the choice to use the story of the Enormous Turnip. To develop their sensory understanding, I might provide compost for the children to feel as the growing medium; I may even have brought in seeds for the children to plant, water and watch grow. Unfortunately, the turnip harvest this year has failed so I am unable to find a turnip in the supermarket. But the story must go on, so I change it to the Enormous Carrot as these are available all year round. To enable all the children in my group to access the story, especially those with sensory needs, there are some questions I need to ask: Do all the children know what a carrot is? Indeed, how many forms does a carrot take? What experience of carrots, if any, have the children had? Have they all seen and tasted one, and if so, what sort was it? I am sure you may come up with more examples than I had room for here!

Fresh from the soil with feathery fronds	Straight and washed	Knobbly and mis-shapen	Baby carrots straight from the ground
Orange, yellow, purple and white, but orange inside!	Carrot sticks	Grated carrot	Sliced rings of carrots
Supermarket bag of pre-washed carrots	Tinned carrots	A plastic carrot!	Carrot soup, cake and juice

For a child with sensory, physical and/or cognitive disabilities to fully understand and generalise what a carrot is, they must have had many different opportunities to experience the different forms carrots can take, using all their senses. Differentiated teaching and learning opportunities provide a variety of different ways of presenting the carrots to cater for children's different learning styles and sensory needs. They need to see carrots, feel carrots, touch carrots, smell carrots, perhaps experience growing carrots and taste carrots in all their various forms. So much for choosing a simple traditional tale as a stimulus! We haven't got onto the family members and animals mentioned in the story, let alone that the carrots were growing in the ground on a farm!

Example two: a themed approach to multisensory learning

The rainforest

For many years, I have used themes as a focus for delivering learning opportunities. In a previous role, I was lucky enough to have an

Table 7.1 Sensory experiences in the outdoor 'rainforest'

	Warm/hot weather	Cool/cold weather	Wet weather	Windy weather
General	Bright sunny days enabled the children to experience that different clothing is worn when it is hot. Shorts and T-shirts are thin and practical as are baseball hats and straw sun hats. As looking at the sun is dangerous we wore sunglasses to protect our eyes from the sun and experienced how dark glasses changed the colours in the environment around us.	Cooler days required jumpers to be left on or coats to be worn to keep us warm. The absence of the sun meant colours appeared less bright, contrast was less defined and the foliage felt cold to the touch. Cold soil feels different and does not have such a strong aroma.	Wet weather provided the most amazing sessions as many of the children did not have the opportunity to experience play or extended periods in the rain. We explored the textures of waterproof materials and then wrapped up in waterproofs, wore wellies and used umbrellas.	Windy days. Wind on cooler days provides opportunities to listen to and watch the movement of grasses and leaves and feel the foliage as it is blown onto their bodies.
Vision	Look at trees, bushes and flowers in the garden, observe areas of light and dark, colours of leaves and flowers, contrasting areas of brightness and shade, patterns created by sunlight shining through leaf canopies, shapes and sizes of leaves, looking through sunglasses.	Look at trees, bushes and flowers in the garden, observe areas of light and dark, colours of leaves and flowers light and dark, contrast, observe the movement of leaves in the breeze/wind, shapes and sizes of leaves.	Look at trees, bushes and flowers in the garden, observe areas of light and dark, colours of leaves and flowers, light and dark, contrast, movement of leaves, watching raindrops falling onto and off foliage, colours of clothing and wellies, colours of umbrellas.	Seeing the foliage sway in the wind, leaves fall and blown along the ground or through the air.
Hearing	Insects and birds in the garden, rustling of foliage and branches, children exploring insects and birds in the garden.	Insects and birds in the garden, rustling of foliage and branches.	Birds in the garden, rustling of foliage and branches, raindrops falling on waterproofs and on umbrella, splashing through puddles, squelching of wellies in the muddy ground.	Hearing the sound of the wind as it blows through the trees and foliage; louder and softer.

Smell	Foliage, flowers, warm earth.	Foliage, cold earth.	Rain on foliage, cold, damp earth.	Different smells carried on the wind.
Touch	Clothing on skin, textures of clothing, texture of sun hat, weight of hat on head, texture of foliage, texture of bark.	Clothing on skin, textures of clothing, weight of warm clothes and coats, texture of foliage, texture of bark, cool soil.	Clothing on skin, textures of clothing, weight of waterproofs, weight of wellies on feet, textures of wet foliage, texture of bark, wet soil, mud, water.	The feel of the wind on the skin/face/body/hair, flapping clothing.
Vestibular	Sitting under trees, standing, moving through the garden whether walking or being pushed in a wheelchair.	Sitting, standing, moving.	Sitting, standing, moving through the garden.	Leaning into the wind; resisting it.
Proprioceptive	Reaching to feel leaves, etc.	Reaching to feel leaves, etc.	Reaching to feel leaves, etc.	
Temperature	The children were able to feel the warmth of the sun on exposed areas of their bodies and how the sun warmed their clothing.	Explore coolness of the foliage, changes of temperature from inside to outside. The drop in temperature when the heat of the sun was not directly on our bodies.	Cold, feel coolness of the foliage, changes of temperature from inside to outside.	Feeling changes in temperature when the wind blows. May be warm or cold.

outside teaching and learning environment which I was able to turn into a discrete learning space to enable my multisensory children to access themes and stories. We had access to a sensory garden which we visited to experience trees, leaves and grasses. Children could feel the bark of the trees and touch, pull, taste and smell the leaves and grasses, either as independent learners or coactively with support. Visits to the garden took place on many different occasions, giving the children many opportunities to experience different light and weather conditions. Most early years settings will have regular access to the outdoor environment that can be developed into a sensory learning space. Examples of how this environment was used to promote multisensory learning are given in table 7.1.

Re-creating the rainforest environment inside the setting

In addition to the outdoors, the theme was explored inside too. Having chosen the area of the indoor environment that would be used, we covered the walls by hanging camouflage nets to represent the thick undergrowth and canopy. Fixed to these were leaf prints, leaf collages and textured leaves we made in our art sessions. Children's work was supplemented by leaves and branches collected during outdoor visits. To add dimension to our environment, tree trunks were fashioned from the inner, thick cardboard rolls of vinyl flooring. The children painted these brown, having previously experienced looking at, feeling and smelling the trunks of trees growing in the school garden.

We placed realistic stuffed animals, such as monkeys, and the children's representations of animals made in our art lessons, to look as if they were climbing through the trees.

Towards the ceiling we created netting clouds from which we suspended rain drops. To make this realistic during our sessions inside, we placed trigger-spray bottles of water in strategic places which we used at appropriate times to represent falling rain. A large sun (an electric lamp) was hung from the ceiling and a hairdryer and fan heater were used on a hot setting, to represent the heat from the sun. Birds and insects were suspended from the ceiling to complete the effect.

The floor of the 'rainforest' was strewn with leaves, grasses, soil and bark chippings, which created a wonderful texture and aroma, especially on warm days. A river was created dissecting the forest floor using blue fabric. When we took the children in to experience the rainforest we ensured that water was available in bowls and trays for the children to experience 'using' their hands and feet. No self-respecting rainforest setting would be complete without sound effects either! These were produced using laptops and CD players.

Once the rainforest was completed we were guided by the weather regarding the kind of rainforest experience we would offer. On hot days, the children would change into shorts and T-shirts, wear sun hats and sunglasses and put on sun lotion. As explorers, they would be supported to follow a trail through the outdoor sensory garden, exploring the different foliage and trees en route, until they came to the indoor 'rainforest'. Once inside they would experience being in the forest itself. On these sunny days, the heat from outside warmed the materials strewn on the floor and the containers of different types of foliage, soils and bark chippings, creating wonderful aromas, which were brought to the children who were unable to access the floor. As the children moved though the rainforest they were given opportunities to experience the sounds made by the river (via CD), whilst feeling the water with their hands or bare feet. Other children used fishing nets and rods to 'catch fish' in bowls. Animal and bird sounds played alongside the river sound effects and other children were supported to locate them in the 'canopy' and up in the 'sky'.

As explorers become hungry, the children tasted the foods found in the rainforest, such as bananas, guavas and yams. Finally, as the rainforest is only rich in vegetation and wildlife because it is so wet, we had the inevitable rainstorm complete with sound effects. At this point the umbrellas and water sprayers were used to great effect. Sometimes the wind direction changed, providing a fantastic opportunity to learn about cause and effect; we quickly learned to move our umbrellas to prevent us from getting wet!

On wet days, the whole outdoor sensory garden could be turned into the rainforest, and the activity was reversed, experiencing the storm first. Children were taken out into the sensory garden first to briefly experience the rain, before going back inside to put on water-proofs. Then, when suitably clothed, we were able to spend more time outside exploring the wet foliage, splashing in puddles and exploring what happens to soil when it gets wet. It's great fun to squelch in the mud when feet are protected with wellies! Lots of outdoor sensory learning could take place before we then entered the inside space, as before, using fan heaters and hairdryers to create the warmth.

Even the children with profound and complex needs enjoyed the rainforest activities, which was demonstrated in their positive facial expression and sounds, active involvement in the activities and on-task behaviours. Prior learning, which involved the children having many multisensory experiences to develop their understanding of each of the component parts of the experience, was vital. Careful planning of the differentiated activities to ensure we were secure with their out-comes and detailed knowledge of children's prior knowledge and skills ensured that children were motivated, remained focused and most importantly, were able to succeed. Repetition of the activities, in the same order each time, enabled the children to also pick up on cues and anticipate what was going to happen next.

Extending activities in the setting

Art/creative work

During visits to the sensory garden, children were supported to col-lect leaves and grasses they had shown an interest in. Back indoors, this treasure trove was examined and 'sorted', according to as many different criteria as the children were interested in discovering. These included; colour, size, shape, length, species and texture.

During art sessions children were encouraged to explore leaves and use them to create collages by sticking leaves onto giant leaf outlines, leaf prints and to choose leaf colours to create their own leaves.

Exploring animals

Visits to a zoo to see the animals whose natural habitat is the rain-forest were not possible, so the interactive whiteboard was used to watch moving and still images and to listen to the sounds the animals made. Lifelike soft toys and models enabled the children to explore the animals, birds and insects at closer quarters. Butterflies and birds were created using paint and craft materials as were two- and three-dimensional representations of other animals.

Exploring foods

The children had lots of fun finding out about the different foods grown in the rainforest and locating them was relatively easy, as many variet-ies are now readily available in the supermarket including: avocados, coconuts, figs, oranges, lemons, grapefruit, bananas, guavas, pineap-ples, mangos and tomatoes; vegetables including corn, potatoes, rice, winter squash and yams; spices like black pepper, cayenne, chocolate, cinnamon, cloves, ginger, sugar cane and turmeric. We were able to look at, feel, taste and smell the foods individually and use them to create simple meals.

Resources: creating a multisensory environment

It is not necessary to have expensive equipment to create a multisensory environment. The aim is to be able to present as many different sensory experiences to the child as possible, so ordinary everyday objects and materials (as long as they are safe for children to explore) that look, sound and feel different are all that are needed. Spending many years working with children with multisensory impairments including additional cognitive and physical disabilities has made me what I call a 'collector' (but which others may call a 'hoarder'!). I've never dropped my habit of going to charity shops, am a frequent visitor to pound shops, and have even been known to look in skips! This hobby has paid off many times over, when I'm asked by colleagues: 'by the way, have you got a –?'. Creating a multisensory area in an early years provision,

Table 7.2 Sensory experiences in indoor activities

	Art	Animals	Foods
Vision	Finding and collecting leaves; looking at colour, shape, size, similarities and differences. Looking through magnifying glasses.	Watching still and moving images using the interactive whiteboard. Looking at toy and model animals, birds, reptiles and insects. Sorting and matching activities using soft toys. Using craft materials; looking at colour, shapes, size.	Watching still and moving images of the rainforest using the interactive whiteboard. Looking at fruit, vegetables and spices in the supermarket and back in the teaching and learning environment. Looking at colours, shapes, sizes. Looking at whole fruit, vegetables and spices, cut foods, peeled food, raw foods, dried foods and cooked foods. Watching foods in blender and other food preparation equipment.
Hearing	The sounds leaves make as they are handled, walked on.	The sounds made by animals, similarities and differences. Pressing switches to hear animal sounds.	The sounds of spices shaken in packets, sounds of blender making smoothies, sound of wooden spoon stirring. Sound of chopping and mashing different fruits and vegetables.
Smell	The smell of leaves and bark chippings, dry and damp, warm and cool.	A visit to a nature centre or zoo here would offer the experience of the smell of animals in their cages or enclosures.	The smell of different fruits, vegetables and spices, whole, cut, raw, dried, cooked.

(Continued)

Table 7.2 (Continued)

	Art	Animals	Foods
Touch	Feeling the texture of leaves, soil, bark chippings.	Feeling the texture of animal toys, and collage materials, texture of paint, weight and texture of painting and printing tools.	Feeling the textures of whole/cut/peeled/dried/raw and cooked fruit and vegetables, holding and using cooking tools.
Vestibular	Moving through the indoor rainforest and teaching and learning areas.	Mark making in craft and painting activities.	Vestibular and proprioceptive: lifting fruit from shelves in the supermarket, cutting, stirring, picking up to smell and taste, putting down again.
Proprioceptive	Reaching to feel leaves, place leaves under magnifying glasses.	Reaching to feel toys, models and other materials.	Reaching to feel foods and spices in their many different forms.

simply means setting aside an area for multisensory exploration with everyday objects that can be changed daily or weekly. Sometimes you may wish to focus on a particular sense, and children can be encouraged to bring in their own materials from home. At other times themes can be developed, as described above.

Conclusion

Children begin to make sense of the world, from the moment they are born, by processing the information received through their senses, and the sensory experiences of daily living help to build up a 'back catalogue' of knowledge which we rely on to inform choices, decisions and behaviour. Some children who are developmentally very young, will continue to experience the world at this level and will communicate and interact through their responses to sensory stimuli. The practitioner needs to understand how to use multisensory experiences to enhance learning for all children.

Further reading

Martin-Denham, S. (2015) *Teaching Children & Young People with Special Educational Needs and Disabilities.* London: Sage.

Pagliano, P. (2001) *Using a Multisensory Environment: A Practical Guide for Teachers.* London: David Fulton Publishers.

Longhorn, F. (2010) *A Sensory Curriculum for Very Special People (Practical Approach to Curriculum Planning).* London: Souvenir Press.

Supporting behaviour

Steve Brown

This chapter will:

- discuss the meaning of children's behaviour, including challenging behaviour

- offer strategies to support practitioners in modifying challenging behaviour

- encourage reflective practice, within the context of managing behaviour

- consider how parents and other professionals can be positively influenced in supporting children's behaviour

Thinking through behaviours . . .

It's not easy managing children's behaviour at any age. Not least children between 0–5 years of age. I have twin boys who are fast approaching their fifth birthday. They are wonderful and great fun and very hard work! In fact, on occasions I have been very close to sitting down with their mother and deciding which one we will keep and which twin will be sold on eBay (only joking.)

Children in early years settings are going through the complicated beginnings of socialisation and emotional literacy. It is easy to forget when faced with behaviours that challenge us that we are dealing with brains that are rapidly developing, children who have highly energised physical mobility and often egocentric attitudes to sharing and seeing others' points of view. Throw special educational needs and learning difficulties into the mix and there will be problems to solve, that often will require staff to be unorthodox or think differently in their approach to managing behaviour.

Specific SEND behavioural concerns

Anyone who has worked in an early years setting or childminded a friend's 4-year-old will have quickly learnt (the hard way) that this age group can be the most challenging of all. Staff working with primary-age children are three times more likely to receive a serious injury. Where are those injuries likely to occur? If you are thinking the shins you are forgiven, but the answer is much higher up the body – the face/head. I think that one of the main reasons very young children, especially those with SEND, can present with such difficult behaviour is that they have not yet developed adequate emotional understanding and resilience to cope with the world around them. Of course, there is the not so small matter of still learning the rules of social engagement; sharing, turn taking and listening. Communication difficulties such as appearing articulate but lacking in comprehension and unclear speech provide plenty of challenges. SEND children need extra time and patience. Sounds simple doesn't it? Sometimes staff think 'He knows what he is doing' or 'She does that on purpose to annoy me.' I am quietly confident that underneath all the behaviours that we can complain about, 99 per cent of children are feeding off their own anxieties, learnt behaviour and adult responses. Children with disabilities can look for attention and any attention will suffice sometimes. A negative reaction can be better than a positive reaction because it usually lasts longer. Evaluate the next time you attempt to correct a child's negative behaviour or challenge their undesired behaviour. I will speculate that you will spend more time talking at the child, over-explaining or disciplining, than offering praise to the same child who is engaging in positive behaviour.

Identifying causes of behaviours that challenge

There are environmental, behavioural and communication audits at the end of this chapter that can assist in identifying potential causes of challenging behaviour, and possible changes and adaptations that are required to manage it.

It is always worth reflecting on possible diagnoses and conditions that maybe hidden or masked. Some children receive a specific medical diagnosis and that is it. There may be more to the child's difficulties. For example, I work in a school for children with visual impairment and within that setting I meet many children that have ASD traits and other conditions that have never been highlighted but are impeding their development.

Help for parents, carers and families

Staff can feel that caring for SEND children in settings can be difficult. Imagine what it is like for parents, carers and their extended families. Supporting a SEND child in their educational setting successfully will involve supporting the parents/carers. I try to consider strategies that can cross over and be implemented in both environments, such as visual timetables. Parents and carers need to be listened to. Invite parents/carers to group workshops to share staff experience and skills.

Conflict spiral

There is a two-way outcome from any issue or situation that will affect the relationship between the adult and child; a negative or positive one. Everything that can be, should be turned into a positive. The more positive experiences we give to a child the more positive feelings and behaviours will occur, which will result in better reactions.

When a child has a negative experience, what reaction can they give? It's what is often referred to as 'fight or flight', and also a middle ground called 'freeze'. To arrive at conflict, a child generally has

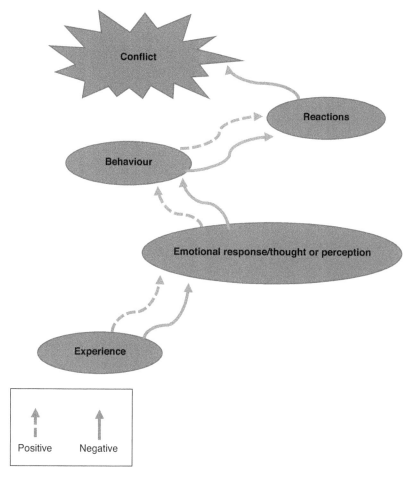

Figure 8.1 Conflict spiral. Adapted from Brown, S. (2015)

to experience a situation which then draws out a negative emotion or feeling which then sparks off a behaviour that leads to a reaction, called the conflict spiral.

If the experience is negative, then it is likely that it will provoke negative emotions and behaviour(s) which result in conflict with others. Of course, things are not always this prescriptive, and the conflict spiral could go in a different order. Any physical responses such as hitting, spitting, pushing, grabbing, biting and scratching have an emotional attachment to them. Generally, if adults are feeling angry there may be a physical action, such as throwing hands up in the air, pointing, shaking a fist or walking away.

As adults, it's important to be careful about how we respond to a child as our actions can either make the situation safer and more manageable, or escalate it further. It is less about the child and more about the behaviour. Remember, it is the adult who needs to stay in control of their own emotions. This will be reflected in our behaviour, which helps create a better chance of getting a more positive reaction over a shorter period of time, or certainly of having a realistic chance of stabilising the situation.

No staff member is infallible. Everyone has the potential to make mistakes. We try to act in good faith and that's the best we can all ask of ourselves and anyone else. Where a child is engaging in challenging behaviour, we can de-escalate by:

- Deflating our body language, moving slightly to one side, reducing eye contact and keeping at least an arm's length away so we are standing in the child's social space. This makes us look more relaxed, calmer and more assertive. It looks more matter-of-fact and less threatening.

- Talking 'slower and lower'. Use simple and clear language and limit the amount of words spoken to help with better processing. More than half of our overall communication is non-verbal, that is, eye contact, posture, facial expressions and hand gestures.

- Reduce pressure and expectation, which will encourage the child to feel less stressed and anxious.

There are not too many times when a child will back down in the heat of the moment; this is more likely to occur when their feelings have subsided and they have cooled down, rather like a boiling kettle of water. Once the water has been boiled, it can take quite a while to start to cool down to a temperature where it is safe to approach.

Promoting positive behaviour through the environment

Creating the right environment that allows children to feel secure and provides positive boundaries is the first step in encouraging positive and safe behaviour. There is a tendency from practitioners to provide overstimulating environments. Rooms and spaces are often cluttered with unnecessary materials. In many cases, display boards are crammed full of words, children's work and pictures. As wonderful as many of these displays look and the immense effort staff have put into them, they can create an overstimulating and distracting atmosphere. Children need space to move around and play, and low-arousal areas and clear spaces to limit the need to constantly process information.

There is no absolute way of creating the perfect environment. In any individual setting the environment will need to be created around the shape of the room and the needs of the children, for example children who may live in a high population density area without access to gardens or their own bedroom, will need and appreciate more open spaces within an early years setting. When setting up the rooms, try not to leave activities out that the children are not allowed to access at any particular time; place a cover over it or a large 'finished' symbol next to it that indicates 'out of bounds'.

The environment can be used to great effect when managing negative or unsafe behaviours. Creating 'nooks and crannies' within the space available for children to withdraw to, can provide a more reassuring place where they feel safer. For example, if a child tries to abscond and runs around the building, climbs on furniture or underneath tables, provide a safe space to move around instead. These spaces and areas could be a tent in a quiet part of the room, beanbags or a specially set-up space with soft furnishings and less of an 'audience'. Try and provide a variety of places so that children can think through their options of where they would prefer to go, or where staff feel is the best place for that child. It is important that any space or room that is being provided is presented in a positive and friendly manner. The best way of supporting positive time out, or withdrawal spaces, is to consider if you would be happy for a photograph of the space to appear on the front page of the local newspaper, on view to the general public.

Withdrawing a child from an activity for unacceptable behaviour is a commonly used strategy, but there can be confusion in terminology when considering the differences between withdrawal, time out and seclusion. To clarify:

Withdrawal: a child is withdrawn from a situation they cannot cope with to another space with close supervision.

Time out: a planned behaviour approach where a child is placed into a space with limited supervision and observed.

Seclusion: a child/person being forced against their will into room/ space that they cannot leave independently. In the United Kingdom it is considered unlawful to seclude a child unless it is an emergency.

Workstation

Some children will feel the need to seek out an individual space in an environment that can be overstimulating, cluttered and confusing. They might benefit from having an individualised space to be supported with play, work activities and communication. Any early setting needs to consider where certain children will need to be situated to support their learning. A separate table/area or 'workstation' in a less stimulating area, with the resources needed to support the child, may be required. The child's communication strategies would also be displayed and implemented there. Staff can provide those spaces easily to counteract noise, disorder and too much stimulation, and offer additional support, such as a visual timetable or 'now and next' board that can sequence and predict what is and will be happening. A 'start' and 'finished' basket may be placed in this area to help facilitate play activities and tasks.

While children in the early years are still learning to socialise, seating plans for particular activities are paramount to encourage appropriate levels of interactions. Sometimes it's important to try and provoke

Figure 8.2 Example of an individual work station

social interaction, and I have invested a lot of time in the past to achieving this. Not all children can cope with involving themselves in an activity and socialising, but the way in which the environment is organised can aid this. It may be better to focus on either activity or socialisation, for an individual child. I usually set up the environment so there are equal opportunities to socially mix and be solitary. Creating space where children can be alone or be involved in parallel play is just as valued.

Sensory integration

Some children are affected by sensory stimulation. In addition to the general environment, the smell of certain foods or personal hygiene products, bright lights or specific textures can cause discomfort or negative reactions. Some children can have adverse reactions from being hyper(over)-sensitive, causing them to withdraw from, and/or hypo(under)-sensitive, causing them to seek out smells, noise, texture, colours and balance, to stimulate them.

Sensory integration tips

- Minimise the amount of stimulation that displays and colours can have on children's sensory processing. Try using pastel backgrounds rather than bright colours.

- Provide safe, quiet and comfortable spaces that children choose or can be directed to withdraw to.

- Complete a sensory audit of the environment and/or an individual checklist, which can help to identify triggers to avoid or areas to support.

- Provide sensory boxes.

- Consider smells and textures in rooms, during activities and at lunchtime – a separate eating area may be required.

The environmental and sensory audit in Appendix 1 at the back of this book will help you to assess a child's sensory experiences.

Positive and assertive behaviour strategies

Starve negative attention – feed positive attention

Spending less time when dealing with challenging behaviour and doing less talking will starve the child of the attention that they might crave when they are displaying behaviours that are undesired. Planned/tactical ignoring is about being very strict and withdrawing attention completely from the child's undesired behaviour. This helps to indirectly discourage the child from continuing to engage in the behaviour.

Forward and back chaining

This has been discussed in Chapter 2 as a teaching strategy, but is also useful for analysing behaviour, by breaking incidents into smaller 'chunks' and working either forwards or backwards to identify the key points at which things have gone wrong. Forward chaining starts at the beginning of an incident. For example, backward chaining could be used when a child throws a block and it hurts another child. Instead of focusing on the injury obtained and consequence, the staff could provide an alternative action with the block which would then prevent a negative outcome.

Positive reinforcement

These are very positive and supportive ways of offering reassurance and giving praise and compliments. A child is playing well or following a request. The adult quickly praises the child and compliments them on what they are doing, for example 'You packed away the toys. Well done'. Making explicit links between acceptable behaviour and praise is also helpful: 'That's good playing/sitting/listening'.

Catch the child being good!

This is an old phrase that has gone out of fashion, but one that is well worth remembering and following. I recall observing a 3-year-old child with a hearing impairment and ASD. When she was perceived to be doing well, no praise was offered, but immediately her behaviour changed to a negative, staff were very quick to reprimand which led to further escalation of her behaviour. When staff changed this, to praise and supportive touch, her behaviour remained positive for longer periods of time and trust was established between her and the adults.

Make a checklist of all the positive words your staff and setting uses to praise and encourage the children. Then establish which words are most effective for which children and adopt them frequently into staff practice.

Positive redirection

This strategy is simply encouraging the child to move on to something else, or distracting attention away from an undesired behaviour, for example, by saying: 'I need your help to finish this puzzle' or 'I have an important job I need help with', at the same time making no reference to the negative behaviour the child is engaged in. This strategy can be used after tactically ignoring the child's initial negative behaviour.

Visual support

Symbol key rings

There are various computer programs that have symbols or pictures that represent an item, a request, an emotion or an activity. Children who are feeling anxious can rely on the visual aspect of the communication. Different colours can be used to highlight the emotions, for example red for angry, orange for sad, yellow for upset and green for happy. These symbols, pictures or photographs can be stored on a key ring and shown to the child to reinforce the message and vocabulary. The pictorial representation can assist in the processing of language. To develop sequencing, two or three cards can be used to help with the spoken word to explain a request or instruction, for example good listening and carpet.

Sequencing strips

This is a strategy that sequences and predicts what the child is expected to do at the present time and then what activities, tasks or choices they will move on to in the near future. This enables the child to see what is coming and ask for additional information, make enquires or verbalise their opinion. Sequencing strips consist of a set of objects of reference, symbols or photographs placed in order depicting the order of activities within a session. An example of two-step sequencing strips

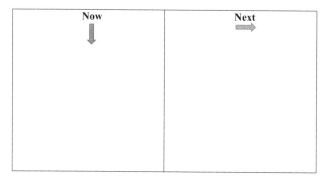

Figure 8.3 Now and next board

is called a 'now and next' board. This is a simple version of sequencing and predicting what the child is expected to do now and what will follow next.

Question marks can be used to indicate possible changes or if the adult is unsure about what might be happening at that specific point in the sequence. Some practitioners find the use of a non-threatening or fun symbol such as a smiling cloud can help the child see the change as more positive. Building in uncertainty to a sequence can help teach a child how to manage changes better. It is designed to support the child in processing the routine, tasks or activities visually. The symbols, photographs or objects of reference are placed in left to right order (the same order we learn to read and write), or can be sequenced vertically from top to bottom, but need to be consistent. For a visually impaired child, staff could record instructions via a recording device.

Sliding scales

Sliding scales or 'salmon lines' can be a very flexible intervention to express or understand emotions and concepts. Sliding scales rely on having two sections to show extremes of emotion. An example is a sliding scale that contains the emotions of happy and angry. The happy half of the scale is represented by the colour yellow which is bright and cheerful. The emotion of angry is indicated by the colour red which is a colour that represents 'danger', 'unsafe' and 'stop'. The number line which runs horizontally from 1 to 10 enables the child to use the numbers instead of words. This can make it easier to express how they are feeling by using the number to represent the intensity of the emotion, for example 'I am a 10 right now, I am very angry!'

Numbers follow a sequence and can appeal to the logical mind of children with ASD. The child can focus their attention on the sliding scale instead of the adult because expressing emotion and talking about feelings can be very difficult and embarrassing. There is a physical action to this strategy by moving the arrow along the number line which can help the child to express how they feel from one moment to the next. The adults can also indicate where they feel the child is, and set a target to work towards. For example, the child is a '9' and the adult explains the need to try and become a '5' because this is a safer place to be. The thrust of this strategy is to demonstrate that extreme emotions are unsustainable and can lead to problems. Being in the middle is safer. Other emotions that have been supported successfully using sliding scales are around being calm or anxious.

Another example of a how a sliding scale can direct the child to understand the negative impact of their behaviour is volume. If a child is being too noisy, then the arrow can be used to show this and then what needs to happen next. I used this with a 5-year-old boy with limited language and autism who would scream every time he did not want to do a task. Over a period of three weeks he learnt that he could scream when he was outside in the playground, but that inside

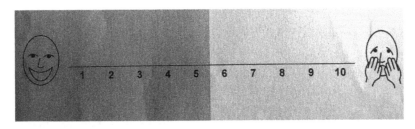

Figure 8.4 Happy–anxious sliding scale. Adapted from Brown, S. (2015)

he needed to use a quieter voice. The simple and rigid rule appealed to him and helped to reduce the screaming and the associated behaviour when staff tried to stop him. The visual strategy helped to focus his attention with the adult. Children with ASD tend to be more rigid and 'black and white' in their approach. This intervention can help to encourage children to think about the 'grey area' by discouraging the extremes of thinking and behaviour.

Task boards

Task boards can be implemented with all age ranges and abilities. A task board is essentially a tick sheet or grid where the child can see the order of the tasks that have been set, where the learning breaks are and when they have finished. The number of tasks or activities that are put on the board is proportionate to how much the child can complete, perhaps three or more. There is usually a tick box next to the task so the adult or child can indicate they have finished by placing a tick inside it. Keeping each task sheet can demonstrate the work the child has completed or attempted and becomes good evidence, otherwise they can be laminated and re-used. Task boards give an indication of when tasks will finish and are excellent for sequencing and predicting the order of the tasks and work activities. They can be used for individual children, small groups or in the whole class. The child can feel a sense of achievement when they have completed or attempted the tasks on the board. It visually reminds them of what they have accomplished.

Supportive and positive physical touch/contact

The use of physical touch is extremely important and staff should incorporate it into their practice as often as it is deemed necessary. Using physical touch can aid verbal communication and also replace it. Allowing a child to hold an adult's hand can send a positive message that they are being cared for. Placing an arm around a child's shoulder can send a message of reassurance. Giving a high five or a handshake can mean more than words can say. Young children, especially those with a SEND, sometimes need physically prompting and guiding to redirect their movement, to become calmer and to support them to disengage in behaviours that involve disproportionate risk.

Times have changed dramatically in the last thirty years regarding physical touch. I can recall having my hands smacked in a playgroup when I was four, and by my reception teacher, the latter for grabbing a spade from another child. These sorts of reactions from staff would now result in disciplinary action. Later in life, it was a feature of my childhood to be smacked regularly by my parents to correct my behaviour. None of this helped. What was needed, was for adults to role model the appropriate behaviour. Physical punishment made me resent the adults around me, whereas a reassuring touch and an assertive word in my ear would have been much appreciated, and more effective.

Positive physical touch/contact needs to be a common occurrence where staff can offer comfort and reassurance to help calm, or move a child to a safer place. Staff should be congratulating children by giving high fives and handshakes. During a visit to a nursey, I crouched to speak with a child when suddenly a 3-year-old boy sprinted across the room and leapt on top of me. I could feel his arms around my neck, his legs wrapped around my back and the dribble dripping down my neck! I spent a minute talking calmly to him, encouraging him to place his feet on the floor and then crouch next to me so that we had our arms around each other's shoulders. I wanted to role model safer physical touch and a more appropriate manner of greeting. He was then able talk to me and I was better able to listen.

Physical restraint

As a last resort, practitioners may feel the need to hold or restrain a child to help prevent self-harming, injury to another child or adult, or damage to property. Again, uncomfortable as this can be to contemplate or administer, it is an important component of keeping children safe. Ideally, a setting should seek training through an accredited organisation that has a sound reputation for delivering physical intervention techniques that always consider de-escalation as the foremost important approach. Training organisations such as Team Teach® offer an holistic approach to behaviour management, de-escalation and positive handling. All practitioners should be trained irrespective of their role.

Tips:

- use safe, friendly and assertive physical contact/touch to reassure children and to reinforce communication, for example high fives or handshake;

- consider accredited positive handling and physical intervention that includes a greater emphasis on de-escalation for your setting;

- establish a 'physical contact' policy that all practitioners and parents are familiar with.

Defiance, opposition and avoidance

These three behavioural traits can be amongst the most frustrating and difficult to facilitate, but it must be remembered that:

1. Any of these three behaviours can be age-appropriate or related to possible diagnoses such as ASD, pathological demand avoidance (PDA) or oppositional defiance disorder (ODD).

2. The adult's feelings can become hurt, with frustration, anger and confusion, which is why these types of behaviours are so challenging. In other words, the practitioner's emotional state is compromised easily when a young child is being oppositional. All three of these behaviours can lead to adult–child confrontation.

3. It's vital not to take these behaviours personally, and to focus on the challenging behaviour, *not* the child's personality.

Strategies to support

- Be aware of your own non-verbal communication. Limit eye contact, engage in assertive but relaxed body language, and non-confrontational posture.

- Simplify language to help with the child's ability to process information. Control your voice so it is calm and assertive, matter-of-fact and lower tone.

- Try not to plead, or ask open-ended questions such as 'Could you pick up the toy please?'. Instead, use embedded commands, for example 'Let's pick up the toys'. Or 'Everyone needs to pick up one toy and put it away'. Or make the request a friendly challenge: 'How many toys can be put away by the time I count to ten?'.

- If the child continues to present as defiant or oppositional, give restricted choices (ideally choice from two with adult-desired choice last): 'Pick up the toy and give it to me or put it on the table'. This allows a child who prefers to avoid following requests to 'save face'. The adult must resist sarcastic comments or a belittling tone, for example 'It's about time'.

- If a particular behaviour persists, then the adult can give other choices, for example 'We can play with the toy inside or outside'. Then switch to: 'We can play on the bikes or in the sand'. The purpose of this scaffolding of choices is to partially control the variables. If the child attempts to engage in other activities, state that those are finished.

- Allow the child to work through tantrums and outbursts; this is not a failure of the adult to manage the behaviour. Children in this state of mind will lose most of their language capability and the ability to process information.

- Help the child to identify their emotions: 'Are you cross about that?' 'How does that make you feel?' This helps the child to recognise how he is feeling and gives him the opportunity to avoid potential confrontation.

- When the child *does* follow instructions or requests, show apprecia-tion, that is, thanks, well done, that's good. This allows the child to feel some element of control so they don't spiral back into negative behaviours (be aware though that some children do not want the reminder that they have done what you've asked).

Note: any of these strategies can involve signing and visual aids such as emotion cards or an object of reference.

- Provide space or a place for the child to go to or be directed to, to allow them privacy and save face.

Supporting play

Play can be broken down into many skill areas, and is a process of learning how to connect, communicate, share, wait, forward think, backward chain, be a part of a team and understand functional use of objects and toys. All these skills need to be practised and refined in several different environments with various people. There are many children who need to be taught how to play and to understand the value of playing, and it is a mistake for adults to assume that all chil-dren are able to engage in play. As children journey through the age/ stage developmental process of play, it is acceptable for any child to drift between the various stages of solitary, parallel, associative and cooperative play. I know several adults who do not 'mix' well with other adults and would usually prefer to be alone or just be on the perimeter of socialisation. So it is a mistake to expect all children to be able or want to engage consistently in cooperative play.

The following strategies can:

- develop good sitting and good listening skills

- teach the concept of start and finish

- encourage shared attention

- teach cause and effect

- promote appropriate eye contact

- increase expressive and receptive language development.

Non-directed play

Non-directed play is child-led. The child plays with his or her choice of activity or toy. The adult's role is to give a commentary of what the child is engaged in, for example 'Fred is pushing the small blue car'. The adult does not interfere in the play, but offers suggestions.

The aim of this intervention is to develop language skills by labelling and to build a non-threatening rapport with the child.

Treasure box

Find a box and place in it approximately five toys or items that interest the child. Set up in a quiet area and place the box by the adult's side with the child on the other side (I sometimes use a mat to define the child's space). Take an item of interest out of the box and present to the child, labelling it and demonstrating the function(s). Then allow the child to engage with item. Allow time to explore. When the adult feels that there has been an appropriate time to play with the item, show a 'finish' card, to indicate visually that the item is finished with, and place it back in the treasure box. Repeat with the other items. It is important that the adult leads and patiently encourages the child to engage. If the child refuses to engage, throws the items or interacts inappropriately then the adult's job is to role model and persevere. The time period for this intervention needs to be limited for a few minutes to start with, building up gradually alongside what the child can manage. Make it fun and interesting. Turn taking using 'pull-back' toys can also be incorporated, as can the use of 'my turn, your turn'.

Start and finish baskets/trays

This intervention is more structured than a treasure box. Place a basket at each side of the table, leaving enough room for a child to sit facing the adult on the other side. Working left to right (in keeping with reading/writing) label the basket to the left of the child 'start' and the basket on the right side of the child 'finish'. Place the activities or work based items in the start basket and then take them out one at a time to engage with the child. Once the activity or task is considered finished by the adult, it's placed in the finish basket/tray. Repeat until the set activities have been accomplished. Again, start gradually and ignore any negative behaviour. To begin with, choose activities that the child is interested in, or knows they can achieve, and then increase the time and challenges over a period of time.

Sensory box

Place a range of items in a box that children can manipulate such as a fiddle toys, Thera putty or spinning tops that can offer some therapeutic assistance. Build this strategy into a regular routine so the child can access it to relieve stress and anxiety. Children need to be able to explore various materials that are tactile-based to aid relaxation.

Motivators

I have never yet met a child who is not motivated by anything, although it can sometimes be a struggle to find what it is. One child I met would typically float around the setting avoiding any staff attempts to engage. I found a quiet place and we sat facing each other. I had a photo of bubbles and showed him the photo whilst blowing bubbles. He smiled and laughed looking at the bubbles and occasionally tried to catch them. Every time he tried to grab the bubbles from me I presented the photo card and said '(name) wants bubbles'. I then blew more bubbles.

After a few minutes, he either pointed at or pushed the photograph towards me and attempted to say the words. I then used a balloon to pass to him and he watched it and then batted it away. Using these two activities, he sat and 'played' with me for 10 minutes. I recorded the words that he had spoken: bubble, balloon, more, again, where, finish. Some of the words were unclear but understandable in a quiet space. Use the child's special interests to motivate and gain attention. A non-preferred activity can then be briefly introduced before a preferred, using a 'now and next' board.

Language and communication

Children on the autistic spectrum may present with particular communication issues. I can recall a 4-year-old boy who didn't engage in any conversation but when his teacher was talking through basic shapes like triangle and square, he named the correct angles and sides of an octagon and other more complicated shapes. Children with language difficulties at a young age sometimes use language by rote. This means they quickly learn a series of responses that they think the other person will want to hear. It is not just the words that are spoken but the context they are spoken in. For example, I have supported many children that when challenged about a negative behaviour they are engaging in will give a programmed response designed to bat the adult away. The words used become a defence mechanism.

Borg (2011) and Burgoon et al. (1989) explain that 55 to 60 per cent of communication is through body language; eye contact, posture, facial expressions and gestures. Approximately 30 per cent of communication is through not what we say but how we say it. Less than 10 per cent is about the words we use.

With many early years and/or SEND children, communication needs to be visualised. The usual order of visual communication is through object of reference, photograph of the object, drawing and then a symbolic representation. Some children will need one variety, whilst others will need a combination of all three. Using visual props, photographs and symbols will aid the understanding and use of language. Most negative behaviours that occur have a direct relation to language difficulties; it is easy to become frustrated and angry if it is difficult to communicate what you want or need and how you feel.

Another important aspect of communication is processing, which requires skills including: shared attention, memory and concentration.

Adults tend to talk too much and too fast when supporting young children, giving more information than is needed and asking too many questions. Children with ASD, ADHD and general learning difficulties are prone to language processing problems. And even children with the most limited vocabulary and expression, can feel the need to mask their inability to understand. I have supported numerous children who can hide behind rote learned responses that fool most adults into thinking they can understand what is expected. Signing provides helpful support for children with hearing impairments and other SEND children, but using visual support, such as symbols, can help in the wider community where other people can interpret it more easily (see also Chapter 6).

Chapter 6 offers some basic strategies for supporting communication, but here are some examples of how effective communication can

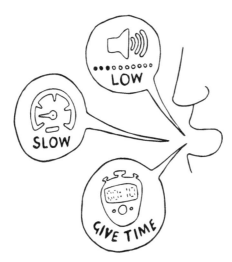

Figure 8.5 Talking low and slow, to allow processing time. Adapted from Brown, S. (2015)

help to shape behaviour. And the 'Communication and behavioural audit' in Appendix 2 at the back of this book will help you to share information on appropriate behaviour strategies and mode of communication used by the child.

Presupposition

With this intervention, the adult is expecting the child to carry out the request or task. 'Well done for sitting down in the chair.' The child had no intention and then suddenly finds him/herself sitting down. Why? The child has been led to believe they have either already agreed to do it or is receiving praise at the start of the interaction and feel it is their idea.

Praise before prompt

This strategy has the same principle as the previous one. The difference is that the praise is used as a 'lead in'. For example: 'That is excellent listening; now let's pack the toys away'. Or 'Thanks for helping; now you need to sit in the chair'.

Again, for children with communication difficulties the use of symbols and photos or object of reference will support the minimal language required. This is another example of a polite, assertive and non-threatening method of encouraging a child to complete a request or instruction. If and when it needs to be repeated, the adult's voice can remain calm and steady, giving a better chance of succeeding.

Delayed compliance

This is a useful strategy for allowing children to process language. Very often the problem with children not following requests and instructions is the use of language and expression from the adults. This is a game of patience. The trick to follow here is to repeat the same words, using exactly the same pace and tone.

Let us consider the following situation: a child who appears to be ignoring an adult instruction to sit on the carpet, but instead is disturbing others around him/her by getting off the carpet and walking around touching other materials in the room.

What often then happens is that after the first time of speaking, the order, tone, pace and language in the instruction can change. For instance:

Instruction one: '(child's name) sit on the carpet'.

Instruction Two (in a slightly louder voice and in a more negative tone): 'I said you need to sit and listen'. The content of the words is slightly different, and the important word 'carpet', is missed out.

Instruction Three: 'Why are you not doing as I have told you to do!' This third statement is not really a request or an instruction and gives no key information carrying words. In fact, it opens the situation up for confrontation.

The most important part of an instruction is the information the adult needs to convey and how the voice conveys it. This includes the non-verbal communication that compliments the spoken words. Delayed compliance is when the adult gives the instruction saying '(child's name) sit on the carpet'. This statement is then repeated three or four times in exactly the same manner, which allows the child to understand the content of the request and follow the instruction. When the same words are said, and in the same manner, the message becomes assertive and consistent.

Take-up time

This strategy is about giving additional time, allowing the opportunity for processing to take place. Take-up time does not necessarily request or make demands from the child. Take-up time is useful to predict and sequence the next step.

Example: adult says, 'Try to put one of your shoes on. I will be back in a moment and help you'.

Example: 'Next we are going outside, put your coat on'.

This is specifically for children who may deliberately be awkward starting a task or have difficulties following instructions. Visual prompts can be used to aid verbal communication.

Holding messages

Holding messages allow smooth transition of communication because the language is structured to predict and sequence what is going to happen. For example, 'children on this table will leave first. Next, children on this table will start to move and find their coat and go outside', and so on. This strategy can be used to demonstrate the content of a lesson, assist with children changing for a PE lesson and getting ready for home time. This strategy is used for giving information to follow several steps that make up a sequence.

Restricted choice

Restricted choice can be very useful for managing children who are challenging authority, want to do something that is not available or have difficulty accepting they cannot continue with a chosen activity.

I want a child to end their turn on the computer. 'Computer is finished (show the finish symbol), you can choose construction or painting'. This is giving the child closed options.

Another way of using this strategy is to say, 'You can choose this . . . or that . . .'. Visual cards or photographs can be used to depict the choices if needed or more helpful.

This cuts out the risky option of the child indicating what they want to do and then there is not the opportunity or time for their chosen activity. The trick with this strategy is to give the best choice last. This is because the choice finishes on a positive note and we tend to remember the last thing that is listed. Give the negative and more undesirable option first so the child can reject it and then present the more positive sounding option that you want the child to

Figure 8.6 Restricted choice. Adapted from Brown, S. (2015)

choose. Start teaching this by offering one choice of something you know they will want.

When and then

This language expression is similar to the 'now and next' approach. It is very useful as it states when something has been completed then another thing can begin. Example: 'When you have finished your work, then you can . . .'. It's a constructed way of indicating to the child what they can do when they have finished the task that has been set.

Positive listening and debriefing

It is fair to state that as professionals and parents, we do not engage in enough positive listening and debriefing after an incident or conflict.

If staff spent more time on debriefing and explaining how the child's behaviour impacts on their welfare and others around them, then a greater level of trust would be established and a more identified understanding of how the adults are trying to help.

Consider the following aspects to positive listening and debriefing: Who is going to facilitate the debriefing? Where will it take place? When is the best time? What materials are needed?

With children who have limited communication, these sessions can be short. Just talking or using appropriate physical touch can give reassurance and build trust. It is not a time to lecture or discipline. This is the time to build bridges.

Become an active listener:

- Use visual aids, objects of reference or signing to support communication.

- Summarise and paraphrase. This demonstrates the adult is listening and checking the details.

- Social stories (Gray and White 2001) are useful to support a better understanding of the desired behaviour.

- The adult is there to reassure and listen, and encourage a better behaviour response. Limit the amount of language.

- Explain the consequences to others and encourage empathy.

- Draw the incident and label what was said by the children and adults. Then re-draw a more positive picture of what the child needs to do in the same situation to help them understand how they can modify their behaviour and responses. It is acceptable to let the child vent and challenge because this is a structured and positive session.

In conclusion, when considering how to approach supporting behaviours that challenge us in the early years, it is worth starting to think how adults respond. When adults remain C.A.L.M. children will benefit the most:

- Communication
  - stance – posture – gesture – facial expression
  - intonation – scripts
- Awareness and assessment
  - reading behaviour – anticipating what might happen next
  - knowledge of handling plans
- Listening and learning
  - give time and space – allow pauses for take-up time
  - give them a way out
- Making safe
  - objects – space – hotspots – safety responses.

There are many components for the adults to consider that support and nurture positive behaviour, such as creating a flexible and well-structured environment, visualising information, limiting spoken language (processing), using transparent and appropriate touch and finally, building trust and openness with children who will quickly work us out, to know whether we care and are occasionally fun to be around. Look at the negative behaviours as tough barriers to remove and always enjoy and acknowledge when children are happy and safe.

Further Reading

Brown, S. (2015) *Autism Spectrum Disorder & De-escalation Strategies. A practical guide to positive behavioural interventions for children and young people.* London: Jessica Kingsley Publishers.

Clements, J. and Zarkowska, E. (2000) *Behavioural Concerns and Autistic Spectrum Disorders: Explanations and strategies for change.* London: Jessica Kingsley Publishers.

Gray, C. and White, A. L. (2001) *My Social Stories Book.* London: Jessica Kingsley Publishers.

Kahneman, D. (2011) *Thinking, Fast and Slow.* London: Penguin Books.

Moran, K. (2012). Research review: The effectiveness of the picture exchange communication system (PECS) on communication and speech for children with autism spectrum disorders: A meta-analysis. *Science in Autism Treatment,* 9(2), 23.

Conclusion

Chris Collett

Putting this book together has been an interesting experience and enabled me to revisit, along with former colleagues from a number of different backgrounds all connected to SEND, what inclusion for children with SEND is all about, more than thirty years after the policy began. Because the inclusion of children with SEND has been part of the fabric of education policy for so long, it can feel as if it's all 'done and dusted' and that there is little more to do. But, as the EYFS (DfE 2014a) reminds us, every child who comes in to an early years setting is unique, and a child with SEND will bring unique strengths and possible challenges. Settings that successfully include children with disabilities, especially those with more complex needs, do so thanks to the knowledge and understanding, hard work and creative thinking of the practitioners, often accompanied by a determination to make it work. In my experience, often the most inclusive practitioners and settings are those to whom it comes entirely naturally to adapt provision for whichever child comes through the door, and for whom disability is seen simply as part of the continuum of child development. These are people who include without really knowing they are doing it. In Chapter 5 of this book, Karen Argent alludes to the ability of picture books to either make 'an issue' of disability, or to have a disabled character presented as 'just another character'. And it is hoped that through the chapters of this book, there has been discussion of the practical strategies that will enable a child with SEND to be 'just another child', instead of an 'issue'.

I have often, during teaching or training sessions, invited students or trainees to come up with what they think inclusion actually means. It is impossible of course to give a simple and all-encompassing explanation, but a word that usually arises – and that couldn't be argued with – is *belonging*. In order to feel included, a child, and the parents, need to feel as if they belong, and as if they have the same entitlement to be in a setting as any other child or parent. In an ideal world, all parents and children would feel that they belong, but the world we live in is far from ideal.

There continue to be substantial barriers to inclusion, not least because of what are often ambivalent attitudes towards disabled people. Progress has been made and continues to be made, but it remains a fact that harassment and victimisation are a routine part of everyday life for disabled people (EHRC 2011), including sustained abuse from those who, in theory, should be caring for them (BBC News 2012). Reforms of the benefit system have rendered the words 'disabled' and 'benefit cheat' as synonymous in the public consciousness, and cruel 'jokes' targeting disabled people are considered to be 'edgy', rather than offensive. The recent Paralympics are often cited as a shining example of the 'acceptance' of disabled people. But even here it could be argued (as it has been by a number of disabled people) that Paralympians themselves distort the understanding of what disability is, and continue to make disabled people 'other' and 'different'.

It was said at the beginning of this book that early years practitioners are subject to high expectations, and inclusion is one of the most important. It is in early years settings that young children begin to develop identity and formulate their understanding of the world around them, including differences of all kinds. Practitioners can help create the blueprint that will stay with children and parents – both disabled and non-disabled – throughout their lives. If the experience of inclusion is positive from the very start, then they will know what can be achieved and what should be expected, and will be better equipped to challenge inequality. So often the key to acceptance is personal experience. Young children, both disabled and non-disabled, who begin their educational journey alongside others with widely varying strengths and needs, and receiving positive messages about difference, will grow into more tolerant adults, who will view disability as part of the natural landscape, in education and in all other walks of life.

Appendix 1
Environment and sensory audit

Date:
Class:
Staff:

Section 1: Physical environment

		Comments/ examples
Displays are not overly stimulating (e.g. not too bright)	Yes/no/unclear/na	
Number of display boards appropriate to the room size	Yes/no/unclear/na	
Lighting good level and in working order (e.g. no flickering lights)	Yes/no/unclear/na	
Room/space layout is defined into specific areas, e.g. workstations, quiet area	Yes/no/unclear/na	
There is an uncluttered space around the whiteboard that displays essential information, e.g. visual timetable	Yes/no/unclear/na	

		Comments/examples
Furniture is appropriate size and room is adequate for number of pupils	Yes/no/unclear/na	
Temperature regulation adequate throughout the day	Yes/no/unclear/na	
Board can be seen at all times, i.e. free from glare	Yes/no/unclear/na	
Quiet withdrawal area available	Yes/no/unclear/na	
Room presentation is tidy and clean	Yes/no/unclear/na	
Are the walls painted a colour that does not distract?	Yes/no/unclear/na	
Are materials stored and organised in a tidy, accessible way?	Yes/no/unclear/na	
Is there a seating plan in place?	Yes/no/unclear/na	

Section 2: Sensory

		Comments/examples
Sensory sensitivities are managed effectively by staff	Yes/no/unclear/na	
Tactile sensory materials are provided to children, e.g. squeeze toy	Yes/no/unclear/na	
Sounds from electronic items are kept to a minimum, e.g. projector hum	Yes/no/unclear/na	

		Comments/ examples
The acoustics are considered and reduced where possible, e.g. carpeted area	Yes/no/unclear/na	
Sounds from outside the classroom are limited	Yes/no/unclear/na	
A sensory room or space is provided for children who need a calm place to relax	Yes/no/unclear/na	
Staff are aware that certain smells may cause distress	Yes/no/unsure/na	
Reasonable adjustments are made for specific children who may not be able to cope with the dining room	Yes/no/unsure/na	
Children who find writing difficult or tiring are allowed to use other recording devices	Yes/no/unclear/na	
Specific sensory equipment is made available if required, e.g. foot wedge, sloping desk or wobble cushion	Yes/no/unclear/na	
A system of support is available for children who experience sensory overload, e.g. learning break	Yes/no/unclear	
Staff make allowances to school uniform to accommodate difficulties with proprioception	Yes/no/unclear	

Appendix 2

Communication and behavioural audit

Date:
Class:
Staff:

Section 1: Behaviour management strategies and organisation

		Comments/ examples
Learning breaks are used regularly	Yes/no/unclear/na	
Visual timetable appropriate and used for individuals/whole class	Yes/no/unclear/na	
Individual workstations used as appropriate	Yes/no/unclear/na	
Rewards are relevant and timely	Yes/no/unclear/na	
Routine for entering/leaving room/ lining up	Yes/no/unclear/na	
Routine and defined roles for tidying up	Yes/no/unclear/na	
Work is appropriate in presentation	Yes/no/unsure/na	
Work is matched to pupil ability	Yes/no/unsure/na	

		Comments/ examples
Sanction and reward systems are clear and understood by staff and students	Yes/no/unclear/na	
Staff in class support each other with behaviour management	Yes/no/unclear/na	
Lessons appear well prepared	Yes/no/unclear/na	
Risk assessments for individual children completed and updated	Yes/no/unclear/na	
Seating plans required and in place	yes/no/unclear/na	
Length of tasks/activities appropriate, e.g. not sitting/ listening too long	Yes/no/unclear/na	
Staff use motivators to engage and/or praise and reward	Yes/no/unclear/na	
Individual behaviour plans	Yes/no/unclear/na	

Section 2: Communication

		Comments/ examples
Specific language strategies used, e.g. restricted choices, presupposition and delayed compliance	Yes/no/unclear/na	
Language level is appropriate (not too much or too fast)	Yes/no/unclear/na	
Use of PECS at break/snack times	Yes/no/unsure/na	
Use of PECS during transitions and lessons	Yes/no/unclear/na	

		Comments/ examples
Use of objects of reference/ materials	Yes/no/unclear/na	
Tasks are presented visually to complement verbal instruction	Yes/no/unclear/na	
Countdown/warning used to support change and end of tasks	Yes/no/unclear/na	
Communication methods are appropriate, e.g. PECS, signing, symbols	Yes/no/unclear/na	
Communication boards in place	Yes/no/unclear/na	
Staff praise communication efforts	Yes/no/unclear/na	
Now and next boards used/ needed	Yes/no/unclear/na	
Sanctions and praise used consistently	Yes/no/unclear/na	
Work baskets used as appropriate	Yes/no/unclear/na	
Task boards are used	Yes/no/unclear/na	
Sequencing strips used/required	Yes/no/unclear/na	
Finished symbol used with verbal prompt	Yes/no/unclear/na	
Finished symbol used to indicate an activity/equipment is unavailable	Yes/no/unclear/na	
Do staff take into consideration the receptive language development levels of the children?	Yes/no/unclear/na	

Section 3: Social interaction

		Comments/ examples
Are the pupils in the class compatible in age, gender and ability/needs?	Yes/no/unclear	
Do the pupils socialise in class?	Yes/no/unclear	
Is the staff ratio adequate to support needs of pupils in class?	Yes/no/unclear	
Do staff initiate social interactions?	Yes/no/unclear	
Play sessions needed to encourage shared attention and functional use of materials/toys	Yes/no/unclear	
Do staff facilitate social interaction groups?	Yes/no/unclear	
Do staff develop independence skills?	Yes/no/unclear	

References

Afasic – Voice for Life at www.afasic.org.uk

Alliance for Inclusive Education (AllfIE) (2010) at www.allfie.org.uk/pages/articles/vol14.html

Apple, M.W. (2004) *Ideology and Curriculum* (3rd ed.). London: Routledge Falmer.

Armstrong, A.C., Armstrong, D., and Spandagou, I. (2010) *Inclusive Education: International policy and practice.* London: Sage.

Audit Commission (2007) *Special Educational Needs: Separation of assessment of need from funding of provision.* Education and Skills Committee available at www.publications.parliament.uk/pa/cm200607/cmselect/cmeduski/memo/specialedneeds/ucm2802.pdf accessed 26th June 2010.

Barton, L. (2005) *Special Educational Needs: An alternative look* available at www.leeds.ac.uk/disability-studies/archiveuk/barton/Warnock.pdf accessed 14th March 2010.

Batten, A., Corbett, C., Rosenblatt, M., Withers, L., and Yuille, R. (2006) *Make School Make Sense.* National Autistic Society available at www.trialogue.org.uk/msms/msmsengland.pdf

Bax, M. (1964) Terminology and classification of cerebral palsy. *Developmental Medicine and Child Neurology* 6: 295–297.

BBC News (2012) *Winterbourne View Abuse Scandal* available at www.bbc.co.uk/news/uk-england-bristol-20078999

Bercow, J. (2008) *The Bercow Review: A review of children and young people with speech, language and communication needs.* London: DCSF.

Berger, J. (1972) *Ways of Seeing.* Harmondsworth: Penguin Books Ltd.

Bondy, A.S., and Frost, L. (1985) *Picture Exchange Communication System* at www.pecsusa.com/pecs.php

Borg, J. (2011) *Body Language: How to know what's REALLY being said* (2nd ed.). Harlow: Pearson Education Ltd.

Borsay, A. (2006) *Disability and Social Policy in Britain since 1750.* Basingstoke: Palgrave.

Brignall, V. (2008) Disability in the Ancient World. *New Statesman.* 7th April 2008.

Brown, S. (2015) *Autism Spectrum Disorder & De-escalation Strategies. A practical guide to positive behavioural interventions for children and young people.* London: Jessica Kingsley Publishers.

Burgoon, J., Buller, D., and Woodall, W. (1989) *Nonverbal Communication: The unspoken dialogue.* London: McGraw Hill.

Burnell, C. (Author), and Anderson, L.E. (Illustrator). (2015) *Mermaid.* London: Scholastic.

Cabinet Office (2010) *Big Society* at https://www.gov.uk/government/speeches/big-society-speech

Centre for Studies in Inclusive Education (2013) *About Inclusion* available at http://www.csie.org.uk/inclusion/

Cheminais, R. (2009) *Effective Multi-Agency Partnerships: Putting Every Child Matters into practice.* London: Sage.

Cigman, R. (2007) *Included or Excluded? The challenge of the mainstream for some SEN children.* London: Routledge.

Cole, M. (2012) *Education, Equality and Human Rights* (3rd ed.) Abingdon: Routledge.

Coleman, N., Sykes, W., and Walker, A. (2013) *Crime and Disabled People. Baseline statistical analysis of measures from the formal legal inquiry into disability-related harassment.* EHRC Publications available at www.equalityhumanrights.com/sites/default/files/research-report-90-crime-and-disabled-people.pdf

Cunningham, C., and Davies, H. (1985) *Working with Parents: Frameworks for collaboration.* Milton Keynes and Philadelphia: Open University Press.

Daily Telegraph (2005) Warnock U-turn on special schools. 9th June. http://www.telegraph.co.uk/news/uknews/1491679/Warnock-U-turn-on-special-schools.html

DCSF (2009) *Lamb Inquiry: Special educational needs and parental confidence.* Nottingham: DCSF Publications.

DES (1978) *Special Educational Needs: Report of the Committee of Enquiry into the education of handicapped children and young people (The Warnock Report)* London: HMSO.

DES (1981) *The 1981 Education Act.* London: HMSO.

Devarakonda, C. (2013) *Diversity & Inclusion in Early Childhood.* London: Sage.

DfE (2011) *Support and Aspiration: A new approach to special educational needs and disability. A consultation.* Norwich: The Stationery Office.

DfE (2012) *Draft Legislation on the Reform of Provision for Children and Young People with Special Educational Needs.* Norwich: The Stationery Office.

DfE (2013) *Childcare and Early Years Providers Survey* available at http://www.gov.uk/government/organisations/department-for-education/about/statistics

DfE (2014) *Children and Families Act.* London: HMSO.

DfE (2014a) *Statutory Framework for the Early Years Foundation Stage.* London: HMSO.

DfE (2014b) *Early Years: Guide to the 0 to 25 SEND Code of Practice. Advice for early years providers that are funded by the local authority.* London: HMSO.

DfE (2015) *Special Educational Needs and Disability Code of Practice: 0 to 25 years. Statutory guidance for organisations which work with and support children and young people who have special educational needs or disabilities.* London: HMSO.

DfES (2001a) *Special Educational Needs Code of Practice.* London: HMSO.

DfES (2001b) *Special Educational Needs Toolkit.* Nottingham: DfES.

DfES (2004) *Change for Children (ECM).* London: HMSO.

DfES and HM Treasury (2007) *Aiming High for Disabled Children. Better support for families.* London: HMSO.

Disability Action (2016) available at www.disabilityaction.org/centre-on-human-rights/human-rights-and-disability/reservations-to-the-convention/

Ekins, A. (2012) *The Changing Face of Special Educational Needs.* Abingdon: Routledge.

Equality Act (2010) available at www.legislation.gov.uk/ukpga/2010/15/pdfs/ukpga_20100015_en.pdf

Equality and Human Rights Commission (2011) *Hidden in Plain Sight: Inquiry into disability-related harassment* available online at www.equalityhumanrights.com/sites/default/files/ehrc_hidden_in_plain_sight_3.pdf

Evans, J. (2009) Creative and aesthetic responses to picturebooks and fine art. *Education 3–13*, 37(2): 177–190.

Farrell, P., Dyson, A., Polat, F., Hutcheson, G., and Gallanaugh, F. (2007) Inclusion and achievement in mainstream schools. *European Journal of Special Needs Education* 22(2), 131–145.

Foundation Years (2016) at www.foundationyears.org.uk/childrens-centres/ accessed 27th September 2016.

Frederickson, N., and Cline, A. (2002) *Special Educational Needs, Inclusion and Diversity: A textbook*. Maidenhead: OUP.

Frederickson, N., Simmonds, E., Evans, L., and Soulsby, C. (2007) Assessing the social and affective outcomes of inclusion. *British Journal of Special Education* June, 34(2): 105–115.

Goodhart, P. (Author), and Tobia, L. (Illustrator) (2010). *Happy Butterfly*. London: Franklin Watts.

Grandin, T. (2016) at www.autism-help.org/story-temple-grandin-autism.htm

Gray, C. and White, A. L. (2001) *My Social Stories Book*. London: Jessica Kingsley Publishers.

Great Britain (1995) *Disability Discrimination Act*. London: TSO.

Haines, S., and Ruebain, D. (2011) *Education, Disability and Social Policy*. Bristol: The Policy Press.

Harris, J., and Roulstone, A. (2011) *Disability, Policy and Professional Practice*. London: Sage.

Hodkinson, A., and Vickerman, P. (2009) *Key Issues in Special Educational Needs and Inclusion*. London: Sage.

Hodkinson, A. (2016) (2nd Edn) *Key Issues in Special Educational Needs and Inclusion*. London: Sage.

House of Commons (2006) *Education and Skills. Third report (SEN)* available at: www.publications.parliament.uk/pa/cm200506/cmselect/cmeduski/478/47802.htm

ICan (2009) *Language and Social Exclusion* (2nd ed.) at www.ican.org.uk/~/media/Ican2/Whats%20the%20Issue/Evidence/4%20Language%20and%20Social%20Exclusion%20pdf.ashx.

ican.org.uk accessed Nov. 2016.

Kalambouka, A., Farrell, P., Dyson, A., and Kaplan, I. (2007) The impact of placing pupils with special educational needs in mainstream schools on the achievement of their peers. *Educational Research* 49(4): 365–382.

Kingsley, E.P. (1987) *Welcome to Holland* available at http://www.child-autism-parent-cafe.com/welcome-to-holland.html accessed Oct. 2016.

Lamb Inquiry (2009) *Special Educational Needs and Parental Confidence*. Nottingham: DCSF Publications.

Locke, A., Ginsborg, J., and Peers, I. (2002) Development and disadvantage: Implications for early years. *International Journal of Language and Communication Disorders* 27(1): 3–15.

MacNaughton, G., and Hughes, P. (2011) *Parents and Professionals in Early Childhood Settings*. Maidenhead: Open University Press.

Martin-Denham, S. (2015) *Teaching Children and Young People with Special Educational Needs and Disabilities*. London: Sage.

Matthew, N., and Clow, S. (2007) Putting disabled children in the picture: Promoting inclusive children's books and media. *International Journal of Early Childhood* 39(2): 65–76.

Meyers, C., and Morgan, C. (1999) Rolling along with Goldilocks and the Three Bears. Bethesda. Woodbine House.

NAHT (2003) Memorandum submitted by NAHT available at www.publications.parliament.uk/pa/cm200506/cmselect/cmeduski/478/6030814.htm accessed Nov. 2016.

NAS (2017) available at: www.autism.org.uk/about/what-is/myths-facts-stats.aspx accessed March 2017.

National College (2010) *Characteristics of Effective Inclusive Leadership*. Nottingham: National College for Leadership of Schools and Children's Services.

Ofsted (2006) HMI 2353 *Inclusion: Does it matter where pupils are taught?* Manchester: Crown Copyright.

Ofsted (2010) *The Special Educational Needs and Disability Review: A statement is not enough*. Manchester: Crown Copyright.

Oliver, M. (1990) *The Politics of Disablement*. Basingstoke: Macmillan.

Quarmby, K. (2011) *Scapegoat: Why we are failing disabled people*. London: Portobello Books.

Reiser, R. (2012) The struggle for disability equality. In Cole, M. *Education, Equality and Human Rights* (3rd ed.). Abingdon: Routledge.

Rogers, C. (2007) Experiencing an 'inclusive' education: Parents and their children with 'special educational needs'. *UK British Journal of Sociology of Education* 28(1): 55–68.

Rose Review (2009) available at www.literacytrust.org.uk/assets/0000/1175/Rose_Review.pdf

Russell, P. (2008) 'Building brighter futures for all our children' – a new focus on families as partners and change agents in the care and development of children with disabilities or special educational needs. *Support for Learning* 23(3): 104–112.

Saunders, K. (2000) *Happy Ever Afters: A storybook code to teaching children about disability*. Stoke on Trent: Trentham Books Ltd.

Stone, B., and Foley, P. (2014) *Towards Integrated Working* in P. Foley and A. Rixon (eds) *Changing Children's Services: Working and Learning Together* (2nd Edition) Bristol: Policy Press.

Talking Point (2016) at www.talkingpoint.org.uk

Tassoni, P. (2015) *Supporting Children with Special Needs* (2nd ed.). London: Hodder.

Tutt, R. (2007) *Every Child Included*. London: Sage.

UNESCO (2003) *The Flagship on EFA and the Right to Education for Persons with Disabilities: Towards inclusion*. Paris: UNESCO available at www.unesco.org/education/efa/know_sharing/flagship_initiatives/disability accessed 14th May 2010.

Unicef (1989) *UN Convention on the Rights of the Child* at www.unicef.org.uk/Documents/Publication-pdfs/UNCRC_PRESS200910web.pdf

United Nations (2006) *Convention on the Rights of Persons with Disabilities* available at: www.un.org/disabilities/convention/conventionfull.shtml

Wall, K. (2011) *Special Needs and Early Years: A practitioner's guide* (3rd ed.). London: Sage.

Walsh, M. (2016) *Isaac and His Amazing Asperger Superpowers!* London: Walker Books.

Warnock, M. (2005) *Special Educational Needs: A new look*. London: Philosophy of Education Society of Great Britain.

Warnock, M., and Norwich, B. (2010) *Special Educational Needs: A new look*. London: Continuum.

Webb, T. (Director) (1992) 'A' is for Autism (DVD). London: British Film Institute.

Welton, J. (Author), and Telford, J. (Illustrator) (2015) *Tomas Loves . . .* London: Jessica Kingsley.

White, R. et al. (2010) *Local Authorities' Experiences of Improving Parental Confidence in the Special Educational Needs Process* (LGA Research Report). Slough: NFER.

Whitehead, M. (2010) *Language and Literacy in the Early Years 0–7* (4th ed.). London: Sage.

Whittaker, J. (2001) *Segregated Schools Must Close* available at: http://disability-studies.leeds.ac.uk/files/library/whittaker-segregated-special-schools-must-close.pdf accessed Sept. 2016.

Wing, L., and Gould J. (1979) Severe impairments of social interaction and assorted abnormalities in children: Epidemiology and classification. *Journal of Autism and Childhood Schizophrenia* 9: 11–29.

Index

academies 24
Achievement for All (AfA) strategy 21
achievement for children with SEND, nature of 58
adults' responses to children's behaviour 166
adults' support, need for 150
advocacy 61
Afasic 123
agencies providing help for children and families 96–8
allergies 149–50
alternative communication *see* augmentative and alternative communication
Anderson, Laura Ellen 114–15
anti-discriminatory practice 27
aphasia 124–5
Apple, M.W. 102
Armstrong, A.C. 21
Asperger syndrome 113
assessment processes 88–9
attention: children's desire for 163; redirection of 172; starving the negative and feeding the positive 170
attention deficit hyperactivity disorder (ADHD) 183

attitudes: changes in 14, 24; of children and their carers 6, 102; to disability 10–14, 115, 191–2
auditory processing 125, 136
audits 193–9
augmentative and alternative communication (AAC) 49, 135–6, 146
austerity measures 91
autism and autism spectrum disorder (ASD) 3, 10, 23, 88, 101–2, 112–13, 124, 128, 130, 133, 164, 174–7, 182–3

baby signing 137
background information on children 27–8, 84; from other professionals 35–6
backward chaining 171
Barton, L. 22
baseline assessment 29
Batten, A. 22–3
behaviour management 162–4, 168, 177–8; policies on 71
behaviour strategies 170–2
Bercow Report (2008) 122–3, 125, 138
Bercow – Ten Years On (report) 138
Berger, John 102–3

'Big Society' idea 77, 80
Birmingham City Council 40, 50
black and minority ethnic (BME)
    communities 109
Blair, Tony 77
Bondy, A.S. 136
Book Trust 116
Borg, J. 182
British Sign Language (BSL) 135–6
Browning, Robert 108
bullying 4, 20, 23
Burgoon, J. 182
Burnell, Cerrie 114–15

'C.A.L.M.' acronym 189
Cameron, David 77, 80
Centre for Studies in Inclusive
    Education (CSIE) 25
cerebral palsy (CP) 10, 124, 128, 149
chaining: of the components of a
    task 46; as a way of analysing
    behaviour 171
challenging behaviour 164–6, 177,
    186–9
charitable institutions 79–80
Child and Adolescent Mental Health
    Service (CAMHS) 96–7
child development centres (CDCs)
    88–9
child protection 76
child ratios 49
Child's Play (publishers) 114
childcare and childminders 68, 84
Children and Families Act (2014)
    2, 23, 27, 51, 83, 138
children's centres 95
choice: restriction of 186–7;
    scaffolding of 178
chunking of information 134
Churchill, Winston 13
cleft palate 124
Climbié, Victoria 76

Cline, A. 14
Clow, S. 111
Code of Practice for SEN (2001)
    18, 26, 63, 82–3
Code of Practice for SEND (2015)
    1–2, 5, 27, 42–4, 39, 53, 64,
    72–4, 84, 88–90, 93–4, 122–3;
    graduated approach of 37, 51, 56
Coleman, N. 10
collaborative working between
    professionals 75
colour-coding of emotions 170–4
commissioning processes 79, 83
Common Assessment Framework 76
communication 121–4; intentional
    and pre-intentional 132–3; and
    language 182–7; methods of
    148–9; non-verbal 132, 166,
    178, 182–7; with parents 69–70;
    pre-verbal 132
communication and behavioural
    audit 196–9
Communication Council/Trust 138
community sector 80–1
conflict spiral 164–6
Contact a Family organisation 97
continuum of need 37
cultural differences 62
Cunningham, C. 62–3

Davis, H. 62–3
deafness 148
debriefing 187–8
de-escalation 166, 177
delayed compliance 184–5
development checks on children
    carried out by health visitors 25–6
developmental coordination
    disorder (DCD) 127–8
developmental delay 31–2,
    35–6, 133
DICSEY code 108–9

differentiation 37–40, 103, 150–1; methods of 38–9
disability: definition of 2; *medical* and *social* models of 12–18
disability awareness 108
Disability Discrimination Act (1995) 2
disability equality duty 103
disability living allowance 5
disability rights movement 14–15
diverity, commitment to 103–4
dolls 116–17
Down syndrome 82, 101
dysfluency 125
dysphasia 125
dyspraxia 101–2, 127

Early Support programme 72–3
early years education 2, 122, 192; formalisation of 6; number of children in 5; *see also* practitioners in the early years sector
Early Years Foundation Stage (EYFS) 29, 53, 84, 90, 93, 191; guidance on 5, 26–7, 29; progress checks at age 2 36; statutory framework for 103–4
echolalia 129
Education Act (1981) 2, 16, 63, 82
Education (Handicapped Children) Act (1970) 13–14
education, health and care (EHC) assessments and plans 24, 39, 51–3, 83, 94; implementation of plans 55; issuing of plans 54–5; reviews of plans 55
educational opportunities denied to disabled people 14
educational psychologists (EPs) 96
emotional and behavioural difficulties (EBD) 19–20

emotions and emotional literacy 162, 165–6, 170–4
empathy 65, 73, 116
empowerment of parents 61–2
English as an additional language (EAL) 131
environment and sensory audit 193–5
epilepsy 13
Equality Act (2010) 2
equality of opportunity 27
errorless learning 48–9
eugenics 13
Evans, J. 107
Every Child Matters agenda 76–7
Every Disabled Child Matters (EDCM) campaign 20
'Everybody In' campaign 115
exclusion: from school 19–20; social 102, 123
eye contact 133, 178

face-to-face communication 70
fading of prompts 48
family structures 59
'fight or flight' reaction 164
finish baskets/trays 181
focus, maintenance of 47
foodstuffs, study of 157–8
forward chaining 171
freak shows 11
Frederickson, N. 14, 20–1
free schools 3, 24
Frost, L. 136
funding 17–18

Galton, Francis 13
generalisation of skills 47
gestural prompts 48
gestural signing 136
Ginsborg, J. 125

Gloucestershire Special Schools
Protection League 22
glue ear 128, 131
Goodheart, Pippa 109–10
grammar schools 25
Grandin, Temple 123, 126
grieving process 65–6
Gross, Jean 138

handshakes 176–7
hate crime linked to disability 10
health and progress reviews 93
health visitors 25–6, 96
Healthy Child Programme (HCP)
reviews 36
hearing, sense of 142, 144
hearing aids 148
hearing impairment 128, 148
hidden costs of having a disabled
child 68
hidden disabilities 10, 101–2, 148
'high fives' 176–7
holding messages 186
Holocaust, the 13
Hughes, P. 61–2
human rights 14, 22
hyperactive children 145;
see also attention deficit
hyperactivity disorder

ICan organisation 98
ignoring undesired behaviour
170, 172
impact of education 19, 25
incidents and incident logs 71
inclusive education 1–2, 9–10,
16–27, 71; barriers to 6, 104,
192; change in meaning of 4;
in the early years 5–6, 106,
119; flaws and failures in
17–19, 21–3; future prospects for
23–5; implementation of 16–17;
policy on 63; positive experience
of 192; rationale for 4–5, 9–10, 71
Inclusive Minds organisation 116
individual education plans 104
individualised spaces 168
individualised support for children
and their parents 59; denial of 23
induction procedures 28, 69
injuries to staff 163
integration in education 2, 15–16
interactive teaching 46
interagency and interdisciplinary
working 75

jargon 90
joint commissioning 83

keyworkers 76, 83–4, 89
Kids Like Me organisation 119
kinaesthetic learners 144
Kingsley, Emily Perl 66–7

'labelling' of children 130
Lamb, Brian (and Lamb Inquiry,
2009) 16, 21, 63–4
language: and communication
182–7; use of 49, 122, 184
language acquisition 131
language development 124
language processing problems 183
'language-rich' activities 135
'lead professional' role 84
learning difficulties 20, 35, 163, 183
learning disability, definition of 2
learning environments 49, 102–6
learning opportunities 147–51
learning styles 144, 151
Letterbox Library 115
listening positively and actively 187–8
local education authorities (LEAs)
18, 52–4, 94
'Local Offers' 24, 51–2, 64, 94–6

Locke, A. 125
lunatic asylums 11, 13

MacNaughton, G. 61–2
Makaton 136–7
Matthew, N. 111
medical model of disability
    12, 14–15
Mencap 97
Meyers, Cindy 118
mobility aids 149
modelling 47, 127, 146
Morgan, Carol 118
motivators 181–2
multi-agency working 74–7;
    factors making for success in
    90–2; for SEN support and EHC
    plans 93–6; and SEND 81–5
multidisciplinary assessments 88–9
multisensory environments 158–61
multisensory experiences 147, 156
multisensory learning 144–5;
    themed approach to 151–6
mutism 126–7

names of children, use of 134
National Autistic Society 80, 97
National Curriculum 19
National Health Service (NHS) 77–9
needs assessments 52–3
negative experiences, feelings
    and behaviours 164–4
negotiating processes 91, 93–4
non-directive teaching 46
'now and next' boards 172–3

observation of children 28–9h
occupational therapists (OTs) 97
Office for Standards in Education
    (Ofsted) 20, 64, 78, 102
Oliver, Mike 12
one-page profiles 39–40, 55

oppositional defiance disorder
    (ODD) 177
outcomes of education 19–21, 43,
    51, 55; factors contributing to
    success with 20; interventions
    and support for meetimg of 45
outdoor environments 154, 156
Outside In World organisation 116
overstimulation 167–8

paediatricians 96
Paralympic Games 108, 192
parent carer forums 72
parent link workers 97
parental consent 89–90
parents: communication with 68–70,
    164; control by 24; involvement of
    57–9, 71–2; lobbying by 22; role
    in decision-making 63–4, 72, 90;
    seen as experts 61, 73; and the
    statutory assessment process 71–2;
    support for and listening to 164;
    see also partnership with parents
participant and non-participant
    observation 28
partnership between the private
    sector and publc or voluntary
    organisations 79
partnership with parents 57, 71;
    deficit approach to 58; different
    interpretations of 69; models of
    63; in practice 64–6; in relation
    to SEND 62–4
pathological demand avoidance
    (PDA) 177
Peers, I. 125
performance-related targets 78
Persona dolls 117
personal budgets 55, 64, 95
personalised learning plans 24
phonics 138–9
phonology 126

physical disabilities 149
physical restraint 176–7
physiotherapists 97
picture books 101, 106–16, 119, 191; complexity of 107; embedded references to disability in 114; examples of 108–16
picture exchange communication system (PECS) 136–7
play 6, 116, 118; child-led 180; support for 179–82
Portage service 98, 106
positive experiences, feelings and behaviours 164, 189; promoted through the environment 167–72
practitioners in the early years sector 2, 6, 9–10, 28, 37, 53–6, 92, 95, 103, 106–8, 144–6, 167, 176–7, 191–2; knowledge possessed by 60–1
pragmatics 126
praise, giving of 48, 184
prejudice 9
presupposition 184
pre-term babies 3
private sector organisations providing services 77–9
profiles of children 39–40, 55
profit motive 79
progress for children with SEND, nature of 58
prompting 47–8, 146
proprioception 142, 144
prosody 126
public services and the public sector 77–8
punishment 176
pupil referral units 3

Quarmby, K. 10

'rainforest' activities 151–6
record-keeping 92

referrals 88–90
Reiser, Richard 108
religion 11
repetition of the same words 185
resources used in the classroom 101, 116–17, 141; organisation of 106; role in establishing a caring and considerate environment 103; seen as part of the curriculum 102; specification of needs 49
reviews of children's progress 49–51, 55
rewards, extrinsic and intrinsic 48–9
rights-based discourse 18, 21
Rogers, C. 19
role-modeling 176
Rose Review (2009) 138
rote-learned responses 183
Russell, P. 20

safeguarding of children 76
Saunders, K. 107–8
'saving face' 178–9
'scaffolding' 134, 178
'school readiness' 6
Scope organisation 97, 116
seating plans for classrooms 168–9
seclusion 168
sectors supporting children and families 77–81, 95
segregation in education 10–16, 22–4
selective schools 24
self-engagement 145
self-image 102
semantics 126
SEN tribunal 63
senses, human 141
sensory boxes 181
sensory experiences 152–3, 159–61
sensory focused activities 146–7
sensory information 143–4, 161
sensory integration 169–70

sensory stories 150–1
sequencing strips 172–3
serious case reviews 76
shaping as a teaching strategy 46
'shared attention' 133
sight, sense of 141–3
sign language 135–6
sliding scales 173–5
smacking 176
SMART targets and SMARTA targets 44–5
smell, sense of 142–4
social Darwinism 13
social engagement 124
social exclusion 102, 123
social model of disability 15–16, 18, 117
social policy 11
social workers 96
socialisation 162, 169
special educational needs (SEN) 15, 18; definition of 2
special educational needs coordinator (SENCo) role 26–7, 37, 43, 50, 54, 72, 83–5, 88–9, 91, 103
special educational needs and disabil-ities (SEND) 1–2
Special Needs and Disability Act (2001) (SENDA) 16
special schools 3–5, 14–16, 20–3, 63, 140; number of children in 3; types of children in 4
specialist teachers 96
speech, language and communication needs (SLCN) 123–7, 130, 138–9
speech and language therapists (SLTs) 97, 135
stammering 125–6
start baskets/trays 181
statements of needs and the process of statementing 15, 18, 24, 51
steps in child development 44

stimuli, responses to 145–6, 161
support devices 101, 111
Sure Start 95
Sykes, W. 10
symbol key rings 172
syntax 126
synthetic phonics 138–9

tactile defensiveness 133
take-up time 186
tantrums 178
task analysis 45
task boards 175
Tassoni, P. 134–5
taste, sense of 142, 144
teacher of the deaf (TOD) role 148
teacher training 1, 4
'team around the child' (TAC) and 'team around the family' (TAF) 82–3
Team-Teach organisation 177
'tell us once' approach 72–3
terminology of disability 2
Thatcher, Margaret 77
themed approach to learning 151–6
time, need for 92
time out 167–8
Tobia, Lauren 109–10
tokenism 103
touch: sense of 142, 144; staff's use of 175–7, 188–9
transagency/transdisciplinary working 76
treasure boxes 180
trial-and-error learning 48, 146
Trussell Trust 80
trust, building of 146, 188–9
Tutt, R. 22
2-year checks on children 35–6

'unique child' principle 26–7, 191
United Nations Children's Fund (UNICEF) 122

United Nations Convention on the Rights of the Child 122
United Nations Convention on the Rights of Persons with Disabilities (UNCRPD) 22
United Nations Declaration of Human Rights 14
United Nations Educational, Scientific and Cultural Organisation (UNESCO) 122

values 6, 107
verbal prompts 48
vestibular system 142, 144
visual impairment 133
visualisation of communication needs 182–3
voluntary sector 77–80

Walker, A. 10
Wall, K. 61–2, 68–9, 75–6
Walsh, Melanie 113–15
Warnock, Mary (and Warnock Report, 1978) 2, 4, 15–20, 57, 62–3, 82
websites 98
Welton, Jude 112–13
wheelchairs and wheelchair users 101, 110–11, 116, 149
'when and then' expression 187
White, R. 6, 82
Whitehead, M. 107
Wing, L. 129
witch hunts 11
withdrawing a child from an activity 168
workstations 168–9
World Health Organization 122